McCALL'S Creates

A Country Home

More than 40 Projects to Make

Margaret Chapman

FRIEDMAN/FAIRFAX
PUBLISHERS

A FRIEDMAN/FAIRFAX BOOK
© 1998 by Michael Friedman
Publishing Group, Inc.

PROJECT EDITOR
Francine Hornberger

ART DIRECTOR
Jeff Batzli

DESIGN
Elan Studio

PHOTOGRAPHY EDITOR
Christopher Bain

COLOR SEPARATIONS BY
Bright Arts Graphics Pte. Ltd.

PRINTED IN ENGLAND BY
Butler &Tanner, Ltd.

1 3 5 7 9 10 8 6 4 2

FOR BULK PURCHASES AND SPECIAL SALES, PLEASE CONTACT:
Friedman/Fairfax Publishers
Attention: Sales Department
15 West 26th Street
New York, New York 10010
212 685-6610 • FAX: 212 685-1307

VISIT OUR WEBSITE:
http://www.metrobooks.com

Acknowledgments

My heartfelt thanks to each designer who created the craft projects in this book and to the gifted McCall's Creates team, past and present, including Peggy Bendel, Lawrice Brazel, Nathalie Cary, Len Eberwein, Barbara Fimbel, Elaine Kiernan, Sean Kim, Linda Novak, Valerie Szurdak and especially Pam May Uitvlucht. My sincere gratitude to The McCall Pattern Company, Bob Hermann, and Marvin Zemel. Thanks also to my daughter Jessica and my husband Stanley for their love and encouragement and to my extraordinary mother, Zella Chevallier Funck, who showed me the power and pleasures of a creative life.

PROJECT DESIGN CREDITS

Kathie Ballard: Tea Towel Bunnies

Joanne Beretta: Homespun Centerpiece, Posie Pillows, Potpourri Dolls, Hearts and Flowers Garland, Blue Denim Dairy Cows, Gingham Cat Nap Pillow, Our Family Fabric Wreath

Victoria A. Brown: Potpourri Sachet

Nathalie Szurdak Cary: Twice Remembered

Lynne Farris: Hoppy Housekeepers

Laure Fedor: Easy Ruffled Baskets

Michelle Hains: Kitchen Bag Angel

Sandra Jeronimo: Potpourri Pie, Fabric Foldie Covered Tin, Plump Pillow Apple Wreath

Claudia Larrabure: Fabric Crochet Baskets, Vintage Yo-Yo Pillow, Country Couple

Pam May: Pretty Pot Coverups, Shade Makeovers

Anne Rader: Apple Blossom Recipe and Basket

Jan Savage: Bee My Honey Gift Sack

Jacquelyn Smyth: Pretty Pot Coverups

Valerie Szurdak: Shade Makeovers

Lois Winston: Coffee, Tea, and Potpourri

Doris Wright: Casserole Cozies, Flower Patch Place Setting

Contents

Introduction

When I was a small child, I used to spend time with my grandmother at her sister's farm in northern Louisiana. When Grandma was cooking, I was told to stay out of the kitchen because it was too hot. When she was cleaning, I had to stay out of the way so I wouldn't get dirty. But in the afternoon, my grandmother would rest. This meant she would sit by the kitchen door where the light was good and do handiwork. Then I could sit on the smooth floor and listen to my grandmother and my Aunt Susy talk about variegated thread, hairpin lace, or starting their next project.

Both my grandmother's and my aunt's houses were filled with wonderful handmade things they made for themselves or had given to each other. Pillowcases embroidered with butterflies, fancy hand towels, amusing pot holders—each handmade treasure had a little story, and if you touched one, someone would always have something to say about it. I can clearly remember admiring a colorful, starched doily with purple and yellow pansies and, in my mind, I hear my grandmother's voice, "Your Aunt Florence made that, she was a nurse." I knew from her tone that Grandma loved and admired Aunt Florence, her handiwork, and her career. Handmade things kept my grandmother and her sisters connected, even though they lived in different states. I never met my great aunt, but the colorful doily made her real to me.

When I was a little older, I was allowed to sit beside the sewing machine and watch my grandmother sew. She gave me a needle and thread and taught me to sew to keep my hands busy. For one of my favorite projects, I made tiny stitches all around a small circle of cloth and then pulled the stitches tight to make a sort of rosette. I've since learned to call these bits of gathered fabric "yo-yos." In Louisiana, they're called *billets doux* (sweet letters) because if you wanted, you could write secret wishes on little bits of paper and tuck them inside the fabric before tying the thread. The scraps of fabric used for making the yo-yos were left over from other things, so as I touched the pretty cloth, I would remember last year's new school dress, or a blouse of my mother's. Hundreds of little circles had to be stitched together to make an airy summer bedcover. I made just enough to stitch into a cover for my doll bed. There are some wonderful yo-yo pillows for you to make in this book: you can enjoy stitching the tiny circles but you won't have to make hundreds of them to complete the pillows!

Making things always presented an opportunity for me to be close to my family, to be talked to seriously, and have my efforts valued. That connection to love and the concentrated attention given to making things with my hands stays with me. Looking at things my mother or grandmother made brings them close to me even now.

There are many different reasons to make things with your hands, to make crafts. My grandmother thought of crafting as a way to rest. She could sit down, take her mind off her troubles, and think only of the pretty stuff in her hands. Also, most crafts can be completed relatively quickly and easily and, when you have finished a project, you have the satisfaction of something to show for your efforts. So much of our work, whether it's housework or our jobs, seems to have no beginning and no end, and often we do not see results. But when we make crafts, we have control of all the choices: when we want to work on it, what colors we want to use, even whether or not we want to be neat. Such freedom is unusual in our everyday activities, as most of our choices are based on financial or other practical constraints.

In my grandmother's house nothing was wasted or thrown away, and if possible it was made into some pretty luxury or decoration. Today we have once again embraced the value of conserving material things, we "reuse and recycle." To me the value of crafting is the same today as it has always been. When I make something with my own hands it carries a part of me. If I take the time to make a nice gift for someone, it's a way for me to show my love for them.

The crafts in this book are some of my favorite *McCall's Creates*® projects from over the years. I've chosen country-style crafts for this special collection because they bring to mind pleasant memories of my grandmother's home. In this fast-changing, high-tech, high-pressure world, I find it comforting to "touch base" with an easier time when many things were handmade. Re-creating this feeling of a simpler life, of a connection to family, and of the pleasures of things handmade is key to creating a country feeling. I hope you'll enjoy creating and decorating with these homemade country crafts!

Margaret Chapman

Chapter One

Before You Begin

Getting Started

This short chapter contains a list of basic crafting tools and general supplies to have on hand before you begin crafting, as well as a primer on glue and illustrated crochet instructions. Refer to this chapter before you begin any new craft project in this book.

Have on Hand

Gather together the tools and supplies you need for crafting. It's a good idea to put them in a storage container with a secure lid, such as a snap-top file box or plastic storage box. This way, you will always have the basics "on hand" and easy to find when you are ready to craft. You will need markers, glues, scissors, and other items listed on this page to make the crafts in this book.

CRAFTER'S TIP

Store your current project supplies together in a box while you are crafting. A plastic storage box with a snap-on lid is a good choice. The lid will keep the supplies inside the box and can also be a handy work surface.

FOR MARKING
- Ruler, tape measure
- Pencil and small pencil sharpener
- Disappearing ink fabric marker
- Black, fine-point permanent fabric marker
- Tracing paper
- Waxed paper
- Poster board

FOR CUTTING
- Scissors for paper
- Small sharp scissors with points
- Wire cutters (or "old" scissors)
- Craft knife
- Awl or nail
- Cardboard
- Rotary cutter, transparent ruler, and mat

FOR GLUING
- Hot- or low-temperature glue gun and glue sticks
- Thick tacky glue
- Permanent fabric glue
- Masking tape

For neat crafting, you will want to have several craft sticks (wood popsicle sticks) and craft picks (toothpicks).

FOR SEWING
- Iron
- Sewing machine
- Scissors for fabric
- Heavy-duty button thread and large-eyed needle
- Needle and thread
- Pins
- Stuffing tool (knitting needle or chopstick)

EXTRAS
You will use these items often if you have them!
- Pinking shears
- Large and small plastic zip-top bags
- Cosmetic powder brush and cotton swabs
- Paper towels
- Spray-on water and stain repellent

CRAFTER'S TIP

Keep one pair of scissors for cutting only fabric so that they stay sharp. Tag your fabric scissors "FABRIC ONLY." Using these scissors for paper and other craft supplies will dull the blades.

GLUE DESCRIPTION CHART

Choosing the right glue to bond your materials can be the key to professional results and a craft project that will last. Many crafters prefer the fast-drying, easy application of hot-melt or low-temperature glue gun. Liquid glue—such as tacky or craft glue—allows more time to reposition pieces. But be sure to add drying time when planning your project. Use a hair dryer on a cool setting to speed drying time.

These are some of the glue products available in your favorite craft and fabric store. Other brands can also work well. Be sure to read the label carefully to find the best glue for your project.

CRAFT GLUE
General purpose adhesive. Wide range of uses. Fast bonding, nonwashable.
- Delta Sobo, Quik
- Aleene's All Purpose White Glue

TACKY GLUE
Use on fabric and most crafts. Dries clear and flexible. Does not soak through. Will wash out.
- Aleene's Tacky Glue
- Plaid Tacky Glue
- No Sew Adhesive

THICK TACKY GLUE
For hard to hold, 3-D items, super thick, super tacky. Not an instant set, but an instant hold.
- Aleene's Thick Designer Tacky
- Delta Velverette
- Delta Thik 'N Tacky

PERMANENT FABRIC GLUE
Permanent bond. Dries clear and flexible. Withstands repeated washings. Some are dry cleanable.
- Aleene's OK To Wash It Fabric Glue
- Bond Fabric Glue
- Plaid Glu' n Wash

ALL-PURPOSE CLEAR GLUE
Use to bond wood, plastic, leather, stones, or fabric. Washer and dryer safe. Perfect for applying rhinestones, ribbon, buttons, and decals to clothing. Do not dry clean.
- Eclectic Craftman's Goop
- Beacon Fabri-tac

GLUE GUN
General craft use, especially florals. Not washable. For hot-melt glue sticks.

LOW-TEMPERATURE GLUE GUN
General craft use. Not washable, except with fabric glue. Can be used on plastic foam. For low-melt glue sticks.

Choose glue sticks made especially for the materials you are gluing. Floral glue sticks dry slower for a longer working time. Fabric glue sticks can be washed and stay flexible after drying. Jewelry glue sticks bond metal, glass, and clay flower pots. The bond stays strong in cold temperatures.

PLASTIC FOAM GLUE
Use to bond all types of foam together, including Styrofoam® plastic foam. Allows time to reposition. Use to glue paper, plastic, glitter, fabric, or wood to foam.
- Beacon - Hold the Foam!™

DOUBLE-SIDED ADHESIVE SHEETS
Use to glue fabric, wood, plastic, glass, and metal to a flat surface. Adheres instantly with no mess.
- Therm O Web - PEELnSTICK™
- True Colors Intl. - STICKnHOLD™

PAPER-BACKED FUSIBLE WEB
Available in 18" width. Used on a large variety of fabrics for appliqués or bonding. Apply heat from iron to create bond. (Instructions vary with manufacturer.) Washable. Dry cleanable.
- Therm O Web HeatnBond,
- HeatnBond Lite
- Pellon WonderUnder
- Aleene's Hot Stitch Fusible Web

LIQUID STIFFENER
Use on trims, doilies, and most fabrics. Synthetic substitute for starch. Water resistant.
- Aleene's Fabric Stiffener and Draping Liquid
- Delta Drape 'N Shape
- Faultless Fabricraft

WOOD GLUE
Use on hard or soft woods. Fast-drying. Super strong, sandable, and paintable.
- Aleene's Professional Wood Glue
- Delta Woodwiz

GLUE STICK
Permanent on paper. Temporary on fabrics. Use for quilting and appliqués. Will not run or bleed through.
- Aleene's Stick Glue
- Pritt Glue Stick
- Dennison Glue Stick

FUSIBLE FLEECE
Use for adding dimension and body to sculptured quilted projects. Layers can be fused together to achieve any desired thickness.
- Handler Textile Corp. (HTC) Fusible Fleece
- Dritz Press-On Fleece

Crochet Stitch Guide

CROCHET HOOK SIZES

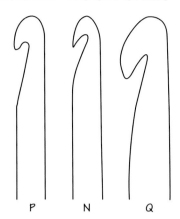

P N Q

SLIPKNOT

Make a loop near the end of fabric strip. Insert the hook, and draw a loop through. Tighten the loop so that it fits loosely around the hook.

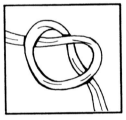

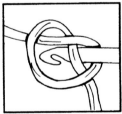

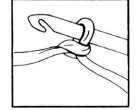

CHAIN (CH)

Wrap the fabric strip over the hook in a counterclockwise direction. Draw the fabric strip through to form a new loop without tightening the previous one. Always wrap the fabric strip this way.

Hint: Keep shifting your left-hand position up close to the hook every couple of stitches or so. This is easy if you use a right-hand fingertip to hold down the loop on the hook while you do so.

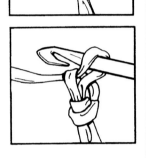

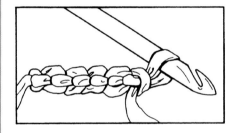

To count chains correctly, make sure you are looking at the front and not the back, and that the chains are not twisted. Count chains from the hook, but do not count the loop still on the hook or the initial slipknot.

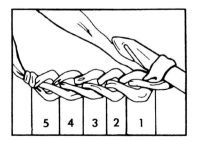

5 4 3 2 1

SINGLE CROCHET (SC)

Insert the hook into the work, or if working into a starting chain, insert the hook into the second chain from the hook. Wrap the fabric strip over the hook, and draw the strip through the first loop only. Wrap the strip again, and draw it through both loops on the hook. This equals 1 sc made.

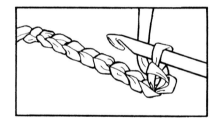

HALF DOUBLE CROCHET (HDC)

Wrap the fabric strip over the hook, insert the hook in the third chain from the hook, and draw a loop though the chain. Wrap the fabric strip over the hook and draw through the 3 loops on the hook.

SINGLE CROCHET IN BACK LOOP ONLY

Insert the hook under one top loop only. Working in the back loop, leave the front loop exposed as a horizontal bar.

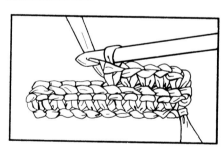

DOUBLE CROCHET (DC)

Wrap the fabric strip over the hook, insert the hook in the fourth stitch or loop from the hook, and draw a loop though. There are now 3 loops on the hook.

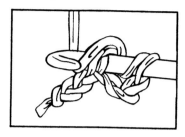

Wrap the fabric strip over the hook and draw it through 2 loops.

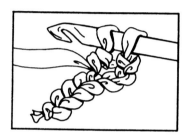

Wrap the fabric strip over the hook again and draw it through the last two loops. This equals 1 dc made.

SLIP STITCH (SL ST)

Insert the hook in the stitch or chain, wrap the fabric strip over the hook, and draw through both the work and the loop on the hook.

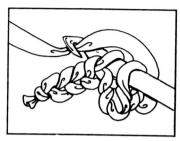

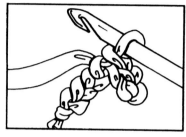

CROCHET ABBREVIATIONS

ch	chain
sl st	slipstitch
dc	double crochet
st(s)	stitch(es)
sc	single crochet
rep	repeat
hdc	half double crochet
rnd	round
*	repeat stitches following the asterisk
( )	work stitches (special instructions)

Chapter Two

A Country Kitchen

Tea Towel Bunnies

This pair of adorable bunnies will cheer up any kitchen, bath, or laundry room. Both the memo magnet and the basket cozy are easy to make by folding and tying ordinary dishcloths and dish towels. Their personalities really blossom when you add an embroidery stitch or two for the face and a bit of ribbon trim. Each would make a wonderful housewarming gift!

Bunny Memo Magnet

YOU WILL NEED

- 6" (15cm) magnet strip
- Small amount of polyester fiberfill
- 20" (51cm) of blue, pink, or yellow double-faced satin ribbon, ¼" (6mm) wide
- Blue, pink, or pastel plaid dishcloth or towel
- Button/carpet thread or heavy crochet cotton
- Embroidery floss in blue and pink and embroidery needle for the bunny's face

MAKE THE BUNNY

① Press the dish towel to remove any creases. Cut heavy-duty button/carpet thread or heavy crochet cotton into 24" (61cm) lengths for wrapping and tying the bunny features.

② Spread the dish towel out flat. The towel's long edges will be the sides and the short edges the top and bottom. Make a ball of fiberfill about the size of a large marble for the bunny's head. Put the ball about 1½" (4cm) below the top edge of the towel, in the

CRAFTER'S TIP

For easy folding and tying, select cloths and towels in plain weave linen, waffle weave cotton, or homespun cotton. Any size square dish cloth will work, as will any size rectangular dish or tea towel. Most plush felt or terry towels are too bulky to produce desired results.

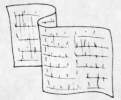 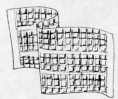 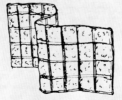

center. Fold the top edge of the towel down and ½" (1.5cm) past the fiberfill ball.

③ Use your hands to gather the towel around the bunny's neck, at the base of the head. Wrap and tie the neck securely.

④ Pull out each top corner of the towel. Wrap and tie each corner near the neck to make a bunny ear.

⑤ Fold each ear behind the bunny's head. Wrap and tie the neck again, including the ears. Roll the ears tighter if necessary, and sew them to the back of the bunny's head with a few small hand stitches.

⑥ With the bunny head face up, gather the entire towel about 2" (5cm) below the neck for the bunny's waist. Wrap loosely, but do not tie. Pull a puff of fabric up from this area on each side to make arms, then wrap the bunny's waist tightly, and tie.

⑦ Wrap and tie the bunny 4" (10cm) below the waist—the area below this tie is the bunny's skirt. Fold the free, bottom edge of the skirt up and around the bunny's body. Wrap and tie around the skirt, over the waist tie.

⑧ Fold the bunny's skirt down. Sew the bottom back corners of the skirt together with a few hand stitches.

FRONT

BACK

STITCH THE FACE

⑨ Thread an embroidery needle with 6 strands of blue floss. Bring the needle from the back of the head through to the front, about ⅕" (5mm) from the center and half of the way up from the neck. Take a ⅛" (3mm) stitch for an eye, and bring the needle out ¼" (6mm) away to make the second eye. Pull thread taut to pinch the face. Take a ¼" (6mm) stitch on this side of the face, bringing the needle out at the first eye. Repeat, making 4 stitches for each eye. Bring the needle out at the back of the bunny's head. Trim the ends of the floss.

⑩ Thread an embroidery needle with 6 strands of pink floss. Insert the needle from the back of the bunny's head and bring it out between and slightly below the two eyes. Make 3 short stitches for the nose, then make 3 long stitches for the mouth. Bring the needle out at the back of the bunny's head. Trim ends of floss.

ADD BOWS & MAGNET

⑪ Cut 6" (15cm) of ribbon. Tie into a small bow, and sew it to the base of one ear. Tie the remaining ribbon into a bow around the bunny's neck. Glue the magnet strip to the back of the bunny.

Bunny Basket Cozy

Finished size: 6"–9" (15–23cm) in diameter

YOU WILL NEED

- Blue striped dish cloth, for basket
- White dish cloth, for bunny
- Small amount of polyester fiberfill
- 1 yd (91.5cm) of blue double-faced satin ribbon, ¼" (6mm) wide
- Round basket about 6"–9" (15–23cm) in diameter
- Button/carpet thread or heavy crochet cotton
- Embroidery floss in blue and pink and embroidery needle for the bunny's face

MAKE THE BUNNY

① Press the white dish towel to remove any creases. Cut heavy-duty button/carpet thread or heavy crochet cotton into 24" (61cm) lengths for wrapping and tying the bunny features.

② Spread the white dish towel out flat. Put the towel's long edges at the sides and the short edges at the top and bottom. Make a ball of fiberfill about the size of a golf ball for the bunny's head. Put the ball about 2½" (6.5cm) below the top edge of the towel, in the center. Fold the top edge of the towel down and ½" (1.5cm) past the fiberfill ball.

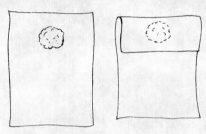

③ Use your hands to gather the towel around the bunny's neck, at the base of the head. Wrap and tie the neck securely.

④ Pull out the corners of the cloth below each side of the head to make the bunny's arms. Wrap and tie each arm about ½" (1.5cm) from the cloth ends to make the bunny's paws. Wrap and tie the bunny below the arms to define the bunny's waist.

⑤ Gather each bottom corner of the cloth into an ear; fold each ear up behind the bunny's head. Wrap and tie the ears tighter if desired, and sew the ears to the back of the head with a few small hand stitches.

⑥ See Bunny Memo Magnet project to stitch the face. Make a ¼" (6mm) stitch for an eye, and bring the needle out ½" (1.5cm) away to make the second eye.

MAKE A BUNNY BASKET

⑦ To make the bunny's skirt, fold the striped dish cloth in half. Sew a curved seam across one corner, beginning 2" (5cm) in from the corner on the fold and ending 2" (5cm) below the corner on the side. Do not trim the seam. Turn the skirt right side out.

⑧ Use long running stitches to gather the other side edge of the skirt. Wrap this edge around the bunny's head, just below the bunny's arms and adjust the gathers to fit. Secure the gathers by making a few small backstitches through the corners of the skirt and the center back of the bunny's

neck. Also sew a few small stitches to join the skirt to the bunny under the arms.

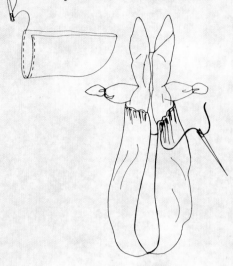

⑨ Cut 5" (13cm) of ribbon. Tie into a small bow, and sew to the base of one ear.

⑩ Thread the tapestry needle with the remaining ribbon. Begin at the center back of the bunny's neck to sew running stitches along the upper edge of the skirt. Do not trim the ribbon tails.

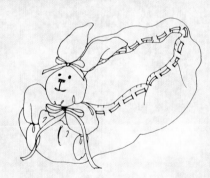

⑪ Place the bunny skirt over the basket. Add fiberfill between the bunny's skirt and the basket if necessary to create a softly rounded shape. Pull the ribbon tails to gather the bunny skirt to fit, then tie into a bow under the bunny's chin.

Potpourri Pie

You can have an appetizing, homemade pie sitting on the kitchen counter, always waiting to welcome guests. The secret of this pretty, fool-the-eye pie is a "recipe" that includes potpourri filling and a felt strip crust, browned with a little paint and crafted in an aluminum pie pan. Serve the pie with a flourish of ribbon and decorative fruit.

Berry Pie

Finished size: 8" (20.5cm)

YOU WILL NEED

- 8" (20.5cm) aluminum pie pan
- 7" (18cm) disposable plastic picnic plate
- Light brown fabric paint
- 9" (23cm) square of blue nylon net
- 4½" × 38" (11.5 × 96.5cm) piece of light brown felt
- 2 yds (1.8m) of dark blue ribbon, ½" (1.5cm) wide
- 2 yds (1.8m) of light blue ribbon, ½" (1.5cm) wide
- 2 small bunches each of artificial blueberries and blackberries with leaves
- Small paintbrush
- Small amount of blue potpourri

MAKE A PIE

(1) Use pinking shears to cut six 1" × 12" (2.5 × 30.5cm) lattice strips and one 2½" × 38" (6.5 × 96.5cm) crust strip from felt.

(2) Cover a flat surface with paper towels. Lay felt strips flat on the towels. Mix paint solution of equal parts of paint and water. Brush solution lightly onto felt. Let dry.

(3) Glue picnic plate upside down inside aluminum pan. This creates a false, raised bottom.

(4) Fold the nylon net square in half twice to form quarters. Pin the straight edges of the 9" (23cm) circle pattern on the folds to cut a circle of nylon net. Unfold the circle.

(5) Glue the edge of the net to the rim of the pan, easing the net upwards to form a dome and stopping about halfway around the rim of the pan.

CRAFTER'S TIPS

- Purchase potpourri with the pie's color scheme in mind. Select blue potpourri for a blueberry pie or brown potpourri for an apple pie.

- Fruit-scented potpourri mixes are available to match the theme of some pies.

- Refresh the scent when it fades by adding a few drops of potpourri oil in between the lattice strips.

6 Fill the pan with potpourri, inserting the potpourri through the unglued edge of the net. Finish gluing the remaining edge of net around the rim of the pan.

ADD THE CRUST

7 Weave lattice strips together in a simple over-and-under pattern, leaving ½" (1.5cm) spaces between the strips. Pin lattice strips together at intersections.

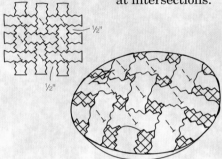

8 Lay woven lattice strips over the net on the pie. Glue each end to the rim of the pan, trimming the strips as necessary. Remove pins.

9 Fold the crust strip in half along its length. Glue the long edges together to form a tube. Let glue dry.

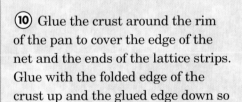
GLUE

10 Glue the crust around the rim of the pan to cover the edge of the net and the ends of the lattice strips. Glue with the folded edge of the crust up and the glued edge down so

that glued edge does not show. Begin gluing at the center of the crust strip, laying a 2"–3" (5–7.5cm) line of glue along the rim of the pan. Pinch the crust into small folds with your fingers. Continue gluing crust 2"–3" (5–7.5cm) at a time, pinching it into folds as you go. At the end of the crust, insert one end of the strip into the other and glue.

ADD RIBBONS AND BERRIES

11 Cut each ribbon in half. Holding one piece of each color together, wrap the ribbon around the bottom of the pan. Bring the ribbons together over the center top of the pie and tie into a bow. Tie the other pair of ribbons in the same manner, crisscrossing the first pair of ribbons.

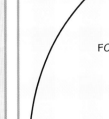
TOP   BOTTOM

12 Glue the bunches of berries with leaves to the center of the bows.

CRAFTER'S TIP

One small jar of fabric paint, when mixed with an equal amount of water, is enough to give dozens of potpourri pies a freshly baked look!

CRAFTER'S TIP

If desired, use rubber finger pads to protect your fingers from hot glue when molding the crust. These pads are available at office supply stores.

¼ PATTERN
FOR 9" (23CM) CIRCLE
PATTERN IS AT 50%,
ENLARGE TO 200%

Homespun Centerpiece

A combination of natural materials found in your kitchen, such as bay leaves, cinnamon sticks, fennel, and assorted nuts are used to create the colorful, rich texture of this rustic centerpiece. Adding unexpected items—some from the craft shop, others made from strips of torn fabrics—will give this project a unique, homespun charm.

YOU WILL NEED

- 2" (5cm) thick Styrofoam circles: two 8" (20cm); one 6½" (16.5cm); and one 5" (12.5cm)
- Florist's spool wire: sizes #16, #18, and #20
- 10" (25.5cm) round grapevine basket
- Torn plaid fabric strips:
  - 12" (30cm) and 36" (91.5cm) of red ½" (1.5cm) wide;
  - 12" (30cm) and 36" (91.5cm) of blue ½" (1.5cm) wide;
  - 36" (91.5cm) of red/blue ½" (1.5cm) wide; and two 12" (30cm) of red/blue ¾" (2cm) wide
- Three 3" (7.5cm) Styrofoam balls

- 6 small dried corn cobs with husks
- 1 large dried corn cob
- About 30 cinnamon sticks
- Bundle of raffia
- About 30 fennel stalks
- Awl (optional)
- Small wood bucket
- Small basket with handle
- Large acorns, poppy pods, walnuts, and pecans
- Wooden spoons
- 4" (10cm) bird
- About 24 red chili peppers
- Bag of bay leaves
- Tin heart-shaped cookie cutter
- Heavy-duty black nylon thread
- Pine brown wood stain (optional)

PREPARE BASKET

1 Stack 3 Styrofoam circles like a wedding cake—in size order with the largest circle on the bottom. Cut 4"–6" (10–15cm) pieces of #16 wire, and bend them like hairpins to wire the foam circles together.

2 Line the grapevine basket with moss. Put the stacked circles inside the grapevine basket. Cover all exposed edges of the foam with moss, using 4"–6" (10–15cm) of #16 wire bent like hairpins to secure the moss to the foam.

PREPARE CONTENTS

3 Wrap long fabric strips around Styrofoam balls. Cover the balls completely. Glue the end of each strip in place.

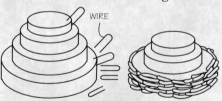

CRAFTER'S TIP

Select fabrics with a quaint, old-fashioned look for these projects. New fabrics that look like vintage textiles are widely available, or you may recycle faded fabrics cut from worn clothes. Another option is to stain fabrics by soaking them in tea; when dry, the color will have soft, antique undertones.

④ Tie a short red and short blue fabric strip around the bases of 3 small corn cobs with husks. To attach the corn to a wreath or Styrofoam centerpiece, insert a piece of #16 wire under the tie. Bend the ends of the wire like a hairpin.

⑤ Trim the husks on the remaining 3 small corn cobs to a scant ½" (1.5cm). Use an awl or a nail to poke a hole near the top of each trimmed cob. Insert 10" (25.5cm) of #16 wire into each hole. Bend the wire ends like a hairpin.

⑥ Cut the large corn cob into 2"–4" (5–10cm) pieces. Insert 10" (25.5cm) of #16 wire through the center of each piece.

⑦ To make 2 bundles of about 10 cinnamon sticks each, wrap a rubber band around the middle of the sticks. Tie raffia into a bow around the rubber band on each bundle. Insert 10" (25.5cm) of #16 wire into the rubber band of each bundle, and bend the wire ends like a hairpin.

⑧ Cut the remaining cinnamon sticks in half. Make them into 2 short, fat bundles with wires. Divide the fennel stalks into 3 equal groups. To make fennel bundles, wrap a rubber band around the middle of the sticks. Tie raffia into a bow around each bundle. Insert wires in the same manner as the cinnamon bundles.

ASSEMBLE

⑨ Glue hazelnuts inside the wood bucket. Glue a few inside the small basket.

⑩ Make several nut clusters. Wrap small nuts with fine #20 wire and twist the wire ends together to make a stem. Wrap the stems with a piece of #16 wire to make a stem sturdy enough to poke into the Styrofoam.

FILL THE BASKET

⑪ Make several small nut clusters. Wrap small nuts with fine #20 wire, and twist the wire ends together to make a stem. Wrap the stems with a piece of #16 wire to make a stem sturdy enough to poke into the Styrofoam.

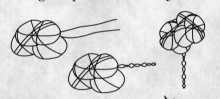

⑫ Arrange the 6 small corn cobs by poking the wires into the Styrofoam.

⑬ Poke the handle of the large wooden spoon into the foam near the basket rim. Poke the handle of the small wooden spoon into the foam near the center top. Glue the wood bucket with nuts to the large wooden spoon.

BUCKET

FRONT VIEW

BACK VIEW

FRONT VIEW

⑭ Cut two 5" (13cm) pieces of #16 wire. Poke them into the Styrofoam to make spears in between the small corn cobs on one side. Stick the basket with nuts and the bird on the spears.

BASKET

BIRD

BACK VIEW

BACK VIEW

⑮ Cut three 5" (13 cm) pieces of #16 wire. Use the wires as spears to arrange the wrapped rag balls. Insert the large corn cob pieces, small nut clusters, cinnamon bundles, and fennel bundles to fill in the large open spaces on the centerpiece. Cut 5" (13cm) spears of #16 wire to add chili peppers in small clusters to the centerpiece. Glue bay leaves to the centerpiece to fill in any bare spots. Glue the cookie cutter near the center top of the arrangement.

Kitchen Bag Angel

A heavenly way to keep plastic grocery bags neat and handy, this angel is not only practical, but will be a great complement to your country kitchen!

YOU WILL NEED

- ¼ yd (23cm) of muslin, for body and arms
- ¾ yd (68.5cm) of fabric, for dress and sleeves
- ½ yd (45.5cm) of fabric, for apron
- ¼ yd (23cm) of fabric, for wings
- ¼ yd (23cm) of lightweight batting
- Polyester fiberfill
- Acrylic paint: green, black, blue, ivory, rose, and red
- Small paintbrush
- Brown marker
- Cotton swabs
- Two 4" (10cm) heart-shape doilies, for pockets
- ¼ yd (23cm) of elastic, ⅛" (3mm) wide
- ½ yd (45.5cm) of satin ribbon, ⅛" (3mm) wide, for neck casing
- Small rolling pin
- Measuring spoons
- 4" (10cm) square doily, for collar
- Button
- Stiff cardboard
- 20 yds (18m) of loopy yarn, for hair
- Lightweight paper, such as typing paper or notepaper, for sewing yarn hair
- ⅓ yd (30.5cm) of wire-edge ribbon, 1½" (1.4cm) wide, for hair bow
- Small whisk
- ⅓ yd (30.5cm) of satin ribbon, ⅛" (3mm) wide, for whisk
- Plastic ring (such as a curtain ring)

CUT THE BODY, DRESS, AND WINGS

① Cut 2 bodies and 4 arms from muslin. Cut an 18" × 32" (45.5 × 81cm) piece of fabric for dress. Cut two 8" × 14" (20.5 × 35.5cm) pieces of fabric for the sleeves. Cut a 14" (35.5cm) square of fabric for the apron. Cut 2 wings from fabric and 1 from batting.

SEW THE BODY

② Use a pencil to lightly transfer the face onto the front of one body section, as shown on pattern. Then, sew the body sections right sides together, leaving the lower edge open. Sew

ABOUT FABRIC

- All seam allowances and hems are ¼" (6mm), unless otherwise noted.
- All fabrics are 45" (114cm) wide.

TRY THIS!

For an old-fashioned look, tea dye the muslin before cutting the pattern pieces. Wash muslin and leave damp. Steep 5 teabags in a cup of boiling water. Soak damp muslin in hot tea for 15 minutes. Remove muslin. Squeeze out extra water. Air dry and press before cutting.

CRAFTER'S TIP

Before sewing the doll, trace the face using this easy trick. Tape the face pattern to a windowpane. Tape one muslin body section over the pattern, right side up. Use a sharp pencil to lightly trace the eyes, nose, and mouth.

over the neck curves a second time to make them stronger. Clip curves. Turn right side out. Stuff firmly. Turn under the raw edges at the bottom and slip stitch closed.

SEW THE ARMS

③ Sew arm sections right sides together, leaving top edge open. Clip curves. Turn right side out. Stuff firmly to ½" (1.5cm) below sew line shown on pattern. Then sew across arm. Leave remainder of arm unstuffed. Set arms aside.

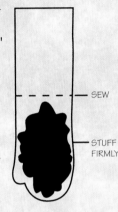

SEW

STUFF FIRMLY

MAKE THE FACE

④ Paint eyes blue or green. When dry, use a toothpick to paint pupils black. When dry, highlight eyes with a dot of ivory.

⑤ Test a brown marker on a scrap of muslin to be sure it does not "feather." Use marker to draw eyeliner, eyelashes, eyebrows, and nose. Outline lips with marker. Fill in mouth with rose paint. Use a cotton swab to brush cheeks with powder blush.

MAKE THE DRESS

⑥ Fold dress piece in half crosswise, right sides together. The seam will be the back of the dress. Stitch from lower edge to 3" (7.5cm) from top.

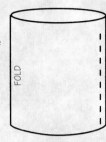

FOLD

⑦ Turn under raw edges at back neck opening of dress and topstitch.

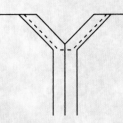

⑧ To make neck casing, turn raw neck edge under ¼" (6mm) and press. Then fold under again and sew close to fold. To make casing at lower edge of dress, turn raw lower edge under and press. Then fold under again and sew close to fold, leaving an opening to insert elastic.

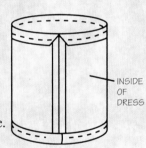

INSIDE OF DRESS

⑨ Thread narrow satin ribbon through neck casing. Put dress on doll, pull ribbon tight, knot, and tie a bow. Thread 8" (20.5cm) of elastic through lower casing. Sew elastic ends together. Slip stitch opening in casing closed.

TRY THIS!

Inserting elastic (or ribbon) into a casing is easy when you attach a small safety pin to one end of the elastic. Use the closed safety pin to guide the elastic through the casing. Remove safety pin.

MAKE THE SLEEVES

FOLD

⑩ To make each sleeve, fold sleeve fabric in half crosswise, right sides together. Sew to make a tube.

⑪ Turn right side out. Insert stuffed arm into sleeve. Pin upper edge of arm just below sleeve raw edge. Sew arm to sleeve side only.

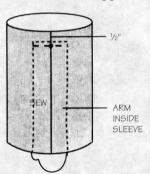

½"

SEW

ARM INSIDE SLEEVE

⑫ Fold in upper sleeve edge, over raw edges of arm. Make 2 rows of running stitches close to folded edge. Pull threads to gather. Knot thread ends.

CRAFTER'S TIP

Sew curved areas twice for strength. After sewing, carefully cut just to, but not through, the stitching line. This will help the curved seams lie smooth.

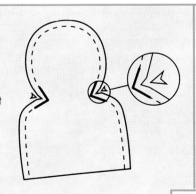

CRAFTER'S TIP

To join 2 folded edges, slip the needle inside one folded edge. Bring it out and pick up ⅛"–¼" (3–6mm) of the other edge. Then reinsert through the first folded edge. Repeat, spacing the stitches ¼" (6mm) apart.

13 Turn lower sleeve edge under. Sew running stitches near folded edge. Pull thread to gather fabric around wrist. Knot thread and tie a bow.

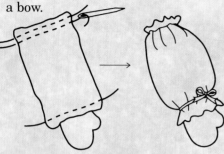

14 Insert other arm in the same way, turning thumb in the opposite direction. Hand stitch sleeves to dress sides just below neck casing to attach the arms. Be sure both thumbs point to the front.

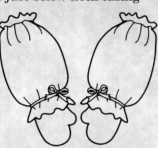

MAKE AN APRON

15 Sew a hem on the sides and bottom of apron fabric square. Fold under 1" (2.5cm) at top raw edge. Sew 3 rows of running stitches close to raw edge.

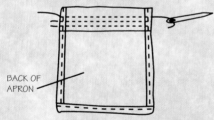

BACK OF APRON

16 Pull threads to gather and knot. Pin one doily pocket to one side of apron. Sew pocket to apron, leaving top open. Sew second doily pocket overlapping the first. Stitch apron to dress front below neck. Place spoons and rolling pin in pockets.

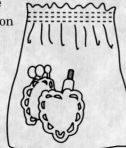

MAKE THE COLLAR

17 Turn under ¼" (6mm) at upper edge of doily. Hot glue at neck edge. Stitch or use craft glue to attach button at neck edge.

MAKE ANGEL HAIR

18 Cut a 5" × 10" (13 × 25.5cm) piece of cardboard. Wrap yarn around cardboard lengthwise 30 times. Secure yarn with a piece of masking tape on each side. Slip yarn off cardboard, but do not remove tape from yarn. Place yarn loops on thin paper. Stitch loops 1¼" (3cm) from one edge, keeping loops in a line. The width of the stitched loops should measure about 6" (15cm).

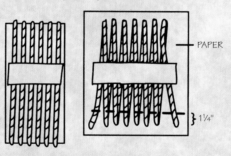

PAPER

1¼"

19 Remove tape and tear away paper. Starting at the center, hot glue hair to angel's head, lining up the stitching with head seam line. Glue one side, then the other.

20 Gather long loops together near top of head and tie with cotton thread to make ponytail. Apply hot glue under ponytail to hold in place. Tie wired ribbon into a bow. Cut a V in the ends of bow. Hot glue bow on ponytail.

MAKE ANGEL WINGS

21 Place 2 fabric wing sections right sides together on top of batting.

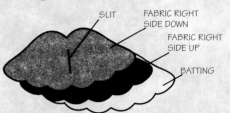

SLIT
FABRIC RIGHT SIDE DOWN
FABRIC RIGHT SIDE UP
BATTING

22 Pin and sew together. Clip curves. Cut a 2" (5cm) slit in center of top layer of fabric only. Turn right side out through slit. Shape edges with the point of a stuffing tool. Hot glue or stitch opening closed. Hot glue or stitch wings to dress back.

FINISHING TOUCHES

23 Tie whisk to arm with ribbon. Stitch plastic ring to back of head for hanging.

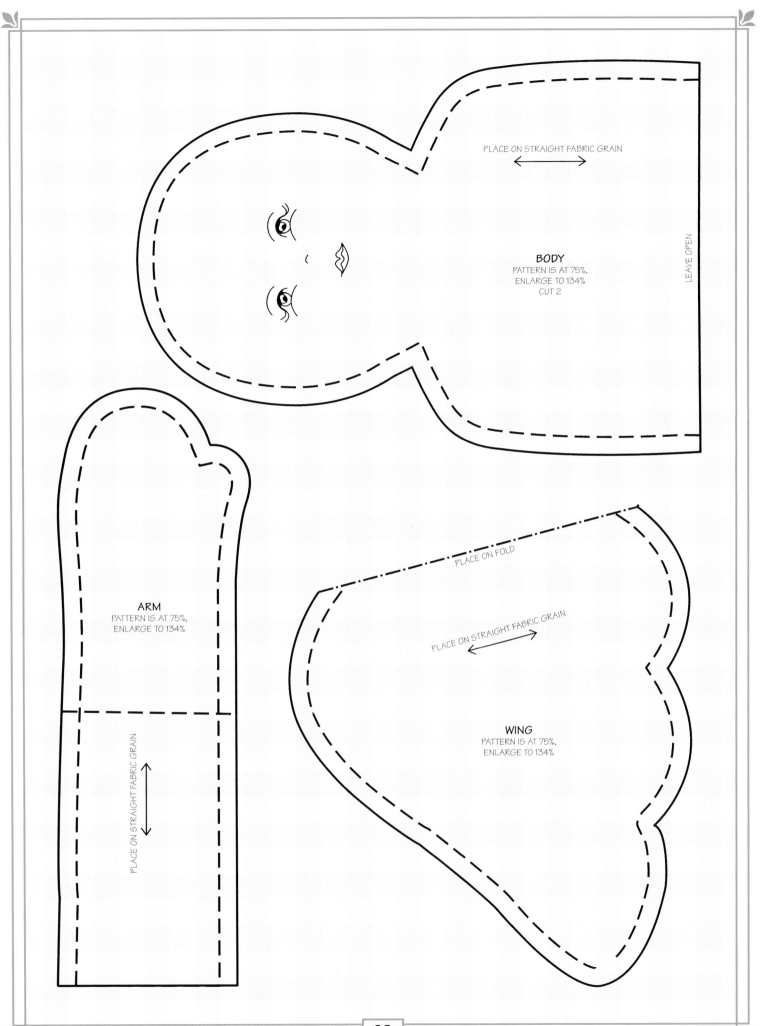

PLACE ON STRAIGHT FABRIC GRAIN

BODY
PATTERN IS AT 75%,
ENLARGE TO 134%
CUT 2

LEAVE OPEN

ARM
PATTERN IS AT 75%,
ENLARGE TO 134%

PLACE ON STRAIGHT FABRIC GRAIN

PLACE ON FOLD

PLACE ON STRAIGHT FABRIC GRAIN

WING
PATTERN IS AT 75%,
ENLARGE TO 134%

Flower Patch Place Setting

Making something decorative and useful from something that would otherwise be thrown out is at the heart of country crafting. Crocheting strips of fabric, also called "rag crochet," is in keeping with this thrifty tradition. These easy-to-make flower-shaped mats can be made from fabric remnants, or you can purchase fabric in colors to match your table setting. The place mats, coasters, and hot pad flowers will bring the garden into your home all year 'round.

CUT THE FABRIC STRIPS

① Each project tells you how wide to cut the strips. You may have to adapt the cut width of the strips slightly for the fabrics you have selected. For example, the lighter in weight the fabric, the wider the strip should be to form a good, chunky crochet stitch. Crochet a sample strip to test the cut width, adjust the width if necessary, then cut all the strips you'll need.

The fast way to cut fabric strips is with a rotary cutter and transparent ruler. Press the fabric to remove wrinkles and creases.

Straighten one crosswise fabric edge by clipping the selvage and tearing straight across. Fold the fabric in half lengthwise, align the transparent ruler along the straightened fabric edge, then cut strips parallel to this edge. Protect the work surface and cutter blade by using a mat underneath as you cut.

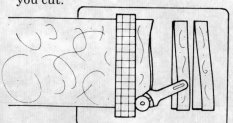

JOIN THE FABRIC STRIPS

② A slip knot is the neatest way to join fabric strips for crocheting. To make this knot, fold the end of two strips over 1" (2.5cm), and cut a ½" (1.5cm) slit into each fold.

③ Stack the strips right sides up with the slits aligned.

CRAFTER'S TIP

See the Crochet Stitch Guide in chapter one for directions on how to make stitches.

ABOUT FABRIC

Use light- to medium-weight cotton or cotton blend fabrics. The amount of fabric needed is the length of strips you'll need to cut. Since the amounts needed are generous enough to cut the strips without extra piecing, you may have some fabric left over.

(4) Pull the end of one strip up through the slits.

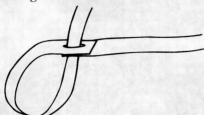

(5) Tug on both strips to tighten the knot.

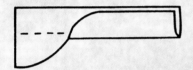

PULL

(6) Fold the fabric strip in half along its length with wrong sides together. Press the fold with your fingers. Wind the folded strip into a ball to prepare to crochet.

Coasters

Finished size: 6" (15cm)

YOU WILL NEED

- ½ yd (40.5cm) of solid or print fabric, cut into 16 yds (14.5m) of 1" (2.5cm) wide strips
- 1½ yds (1.4m) of contrast fabric, cut into 60 yds (55m) of 1" (2.5cm) wide strips
- Crochet hook, size N
- Twist tie or safety pin

(1) Use a solid or print fabric to form a slip knot on hook. Ch 5, join with sl st in first ch to form a ring.

(2) RND 1: Ch 2 (counts as first dc). Mark 2nd ch with a twist tie or safety pin. Working in back loops only throughout, work 2 dc in each of next 4 ch, 3 dc in last ch, join with sl st in marked ch—12sts. Cut the fabric strip. Join contrast fabric strip with sl st in marked ch.

(3) RND 2: Ch 2, mark as in rnd 1, work 2 dc in each of next 10 sts, 3 dc in next st, skip last st, join with sl st in marked ch—24 sts.

(4) RND 3: * Work 2 dc in next st, ch 2, 2 dc in next st, sl st in next st; rep from * around. Cut the fabric strip and weave in the end.

(5) Repeat steps 1 through 4 for each coaster.

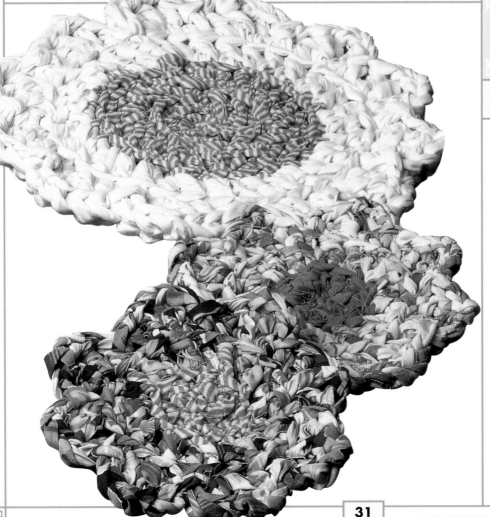

Hot Pad

Finished size: 12" (30.5cm)

YOU WILL NEED

- 1 yd (91.5cm) of striped fabric, cut into 16 yds (14.5m) of 2" (5cm) wide strips
- 2 yds (1.8m) of dotted fabric, cut into 32 yds (29m) of 2" (5cm) wide strips
- Crochet hook, size P
- Twist tie or safety pin

(1) Use a striped fabric strip to form a slipknot on hook. Ch 5, join with sl st in first ch to form a ring.

(2) RND 1: Ch 2 (counts as first dc), mark 2nd ch with a twist tie or safety pin. Working in back loops only throughout, work 2 dc in each of next 4 ch, 3 dc in last ch, join with sl st in marked ch—12 sts.

(3) RND 2: Ch 2, mark as in rnd 1, work 2 dc in each of next 10 sts, 3 dc in next st, skip last st, join with sl st in marked ch—24 sts. Cut the fabric strip. Join dotted fabric strip with sl st in marked ch.

(4) RND 3: Ch 2, mark as in rnd 1, * work 2 dc in next st, 1 dc in next st; rep from * to last st, skip last st, join with sl st in marked ch—36 sts.

(5) RND 4: * Work 2 dc in next st, ch 2, 2 dc in next st, sl st in next st; rep from * around. Cut fabric strip, and weave in the end.

Place Mat

Finished size: 16" (40.5cm)

YOU WILL NEED

- 1 yd (91.5cm) each of 2 colors of fabric, cut into 16 yds (14.5m) of 2" (5cm) wide strips
- 2 yds (1.8m) of contrast fabric, cut into 45 yds (41m) of 2" (5cm) wide strips
- Crochet hook, size Q
- Twist tie or safety pin

(1) Use one color of fabric strip to form a slipknot on hook. Ch 5, join with sl st in first ch to form a ring.

(2) RND 1: Ch 2 (counts as first dc), mark 2nd ch with a twist tie or safety pin. Working in back loops only throughout, work 2 dc in each of next 4 ch, 3 dc in last ch, join with sl st in marked ch—12 sts.

(3) RND 2: Ch 2, mark as in rnd 1, work 2 dc in each of next 10 sts, 3 dc in next st, skip last st, join with sl st in marked ch—24 sts. Cut the fabric strip. Join the other color fabric strip with sl st in marked ch.

(4) RND 3: Ch 2, mark as in rnd 1, * work 2 dc in next st, 1 dc in next st; rep from * 10 times, work 2 dc in next st, skip last st, join with sl st in marked ch—36 sts. Cut the fabric strip. Join a contrast fabric strip with sl st in marked ch.

(5) RND 4: Ch 2, mark as in rnd 1, * work 2 dc in next st, 1 dc in each of next 2 sts; rep from * 10 times, 2 dc in next st, dc in next st, skip last st, join with sl st in marked ch—48 sts.

(6) RND 5: * Work 2 hdc in next st, ch 2, 2 hdc in next st, sl st in next st; rep from * around. Cut the fabric strip, and weave in the end.

Casserole Cozies

You can dress up your favorite potluck supper dish with a country-style casserole cover that will keep your casserole piping hot or muffins warm while the thick texture protects the tabletop. Cut sunny, coordinated print fabrics into strips and crochet them with a Q-hook to make these charming cozies. Accented by natural raffia, they will also make handsome baskets to hold napkins or utensils.

Baking Dish Cozy

Finished cozy fits a standard-size 9" × 12" glass baking dish

YOU WILL NEED

- 6 yds (5.5m) of checked fabric, cut into 75 yds (68.5m) of 3½" (9cm) wide strips
- Crochet hook, size Q
- Twist ties or safety pins
- 1 yd (91.5cm) print fabric, cut into 12 yds (11m) of 3½" (9cm) wide strips
- 1 yd (91.5cm) of household string
- Eight 36" (91.5cm) strands of raffia

CROCHET A COZY

① Form a slipknot on hook using the checked strip. Ch 6, join with sl st in first ch to form a ring.

② RND 1: * Work sc in next st, ch 1; rep from * around—12 sts. Do not join first 2 rnds, but mark end of rnd with a twist tie or safety pin after last st worked, and move it up rnds as work proceeds.

③ RND 2: Working in back loops only, * work sc in next st, ch 1; rep from * around, mark as in rnd 1. Join with sl st in marked st—24 sts.

④ RND 3: Working in back loops only, * work 1 sc in each of next 2 sts, work 2 sc in next st, work 1 sc in each of next 8 sts, work 2 sc in next st; rep from * once. Join with sl st in beg sc—28 sts.

⑤ RND 4: Ch 1 (counts as 1 sc), mark ch—1 with a twist tie or safety pin. Working in back loops only, work 1 sc in next st, 2 sc in next st, ch 1, work 2 sc in next st, sc in each of next 8 sts, work 2 sc in next st, ch 1, 2 sc in next st, sc in each of next 2 sts, 2 sc in next st, ch 1, 2 sc in next st, sc in each

CRAFTER'S TIP

Purchase light- to medium-weight cotton or cotton blend fabrics to cut the strips for rag crochet. Note that the fabric estimates are generous to prevent excessive joining of the strips, so you may have some fabric left over.

CRAFTER'S TIP

Refer to page 30 for directions on how to cut the fabric strips. See the Crochet Stitch Guide in chapter one for directions on how to cut the fabric strips and make stitches.

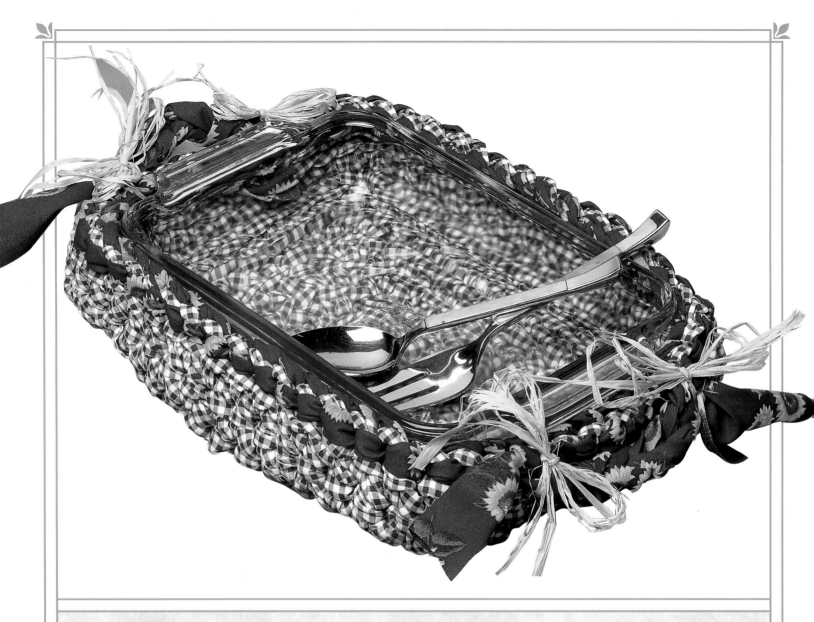

of next 8 sts, 2 sc in next st, ch 1, work 2 sc in next st. Join with sl st in marked st—40 sts.

⑥ RND 5: Ch 1, mark as in rnd 4, working in back loops, work 1 sc in each of next 3 sts, work 2 sc in next st, sc in each of next 12 sts, 2 sc in next st, sc in each of next 6 sts, 2 sc in next st, sc in each of next 12 sts, 2 sc in next st, sc in each of next 2 sts. Join with sl st in marked st—44 sts.

⑦ RND 6: Ch 1, mark as in rnd 4, working in back loops only on remaining rnds, sc in each of next 3 sts, 2 sc in each of next 2 sts, sc in each of next 12 sts, 2 sc in each of next 2 sts, sc in each of next 6 sts, 2 sc in each of next 2 sts, sc in each of next 12 sts, 2 sc in each of

next 2 sts, sc in each of next 2 sts. Join with sl st in marked st—52 sts.

⑧ RND 7: Ch 1, mark as in rnd 4. Working in both loops, sc in each st around. Join with sl st in marked st.

⑨ RND 8: Ch 1, mark as in rnd 4. Working in back loop only on last 2 reds, sc in each st around. Cut the fabric strip. Join contrast fabric strip with sl st in marked st.

⑩ Sl st in each st around basket. Cut the fabric strip, and weave in the end.

⑪ Make a slipknot and ch 9 using the contrast fabric strip for each handle. Cut the fabric strip, and weave in the end.

⑫ Cut four 9" (23cm) pieces of string. Thread each string through a tapestry needle to weave the string through each end of each handle and the fourth st from each corner along an 11" (28cm) side of the basket. Tie each string in a tight knot, and trim the tails. To cover the string, rep with two 18" (45.5cm) strands of raffia. Tie each pair of raffia strands into a bow. Trim the ends of the strands.

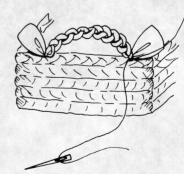

Round Cozy

Finished cozy fits a 9" deep-dish pie plate

YOU WILL NEED

- 4½ yds (4m) of print fabric, cut into 56 yds (51m) of 3½" (9cm) wide strips
- 1 yd (1m) of contrast fabric, cut into 10 yds (9m) of 3½" (9cm) wide strips
- Twelve 15" (38cm) strands of raffia
- Small piece of household string
- Crochet hook, size Q
- Twist ties or safety pins

CROCHET A COZY

① Form a slipknot on hook using print fabric strip. Ch 6, join with sl st in first ch to form a ring.

② RND 1: Ch 2 (counts as 1 dc). Mark last ch of ch-2 with a twist tie or safety pin. Working in back loops only unless otherwise indicated, work 2 dc in each of next 4 ch, 3 dc in next ch, skip next ch. Join with sl st in marked ch—12 sts.

③ RND 2: Ch 2, mark as in Rnd 1. Work 2 dc in each of next 10 sts, 3 dc in next st, skip next st, join with sl st in marked ch—24 sts.

④ RND 3: Ch 1 (counts as 1 sc), mark as in Rnd 1, * work 2 sc in next st, work 1 sc in next st; rep from * around. Join with sl st in marked ch—36 sts.

⑤ RND 4: Ch 2, mark as in Rnd 1, work 2 dc in next st, dc in each of next 5 sts; rep from * 4 times more, work 2 dc in next st, dc in each of next 4 sts, skip next st.

Join with sl st in marked ch—42 sts. Cut the fabric strip. Join contrast fabric strip with sl st in marked ch.

⑥ RND 5: Sl st in each st around. Cut the fabric strip, and weave in the end.

MAKE BOWS

⑦ Cut two 15" (38cm) strips from the contrast fabric strip. Pull one 15" (38cm) strip through any sl along last rnd on opposite sides of the basket.

⑧ Make 2 raffia bows. For each bow, fold six 15" (38cm) strands of raffia into thirds, and pinch at the center. Tie the center with a piece of string. Trim the string tails. Tie each fabric strip around a raffia bow, covering the string.

⑨ Fanfold the end of each fabric strip. Cut diagonally across the folds to make a sawtooth edge.

Fabric Crochet Baskets

Fabric crochet is fast, fun, and easy to do! Choose fabrics for color, as patterns will be changed when cut into strips and "knotted" with the crochet stitches. But checks, prints, and stripes will all work well. Once you've made one of these handy little baskets, you'll be "hooked" and want to make many more for all sorts of uses...for bread, as flowerpot covers, for guest towels, or even for house keys.

Round Basket

YOU WILL NEED

- 2½ yds (2.3m) of lightweight fabric, 54" (1.4m) wide, cut into 3" (7.5cm) wide strips
- Crochet hook, size Q
- Large blunt needle or smaller crochet hook

CROCHET A BASKET

① Form a slipknot on hook. Ch 4, join with a sl st in first ch to form ring.

② RND 1: Next work 2 sc in each of 4 ch sts, working in outside loop only—8 sts. Mark end of rnd with a piece of string or twist tie.

③ RND 2: 2 sc in each sc; work in both loops unless otherwise noted—16 sts.

④ RND 3: * 1 sc in next sc, 2 sc in next sc; rep from * 7 times—24 sts.

⑤ RND 4, 5, 6: 1 sc in each sc; mark end of each rnd; turn basket right side out and shape. Sl st in back loop of next 2 sc—24 sts. Do not cut fabric.

CROCHET THE HANDLE

⑥ Ch 15, extend chain across to opposite edge of basket; remove hook; draw last st of chain through top loops of sc from outside of basket; fabric over and draw through last st in ch, sl st in each ch back to beginning of ch.

⑦ Cut fabric and weave ends into basket with a large blunt needle or smaller crochet hook.

CRAFTER'S TIP

Refer to page 30 for directions on how to cut fabric strips.
See the Crochet Stitch Guide in chapter one for directions on making stitches.

Oval Basket

YOU WILL NEED

- 3½ yds (3m) of fabric, cut into 54" (1.4m) of 3" (7.5cm) wide strips
- Crochet hook, size Q
- Large blunt needle or smaller crochet hook

CROCHET A BASKET

(1) Use fabric strip to make a slipknot on hook. Ch 6, 3 sc in second ch from hook, 1 sc in one side of next 3 ch sts, 3 sc in next ch, working back along opposite side of ch, 1 sc in each of next 3 ch. Mark end of rnd—12 sts.

(2) Rnd 2: 3 sc in next sc, 1 sc in next sc, 3 sc in next sc, 1 sc in each of next 3 sc, 3 sc in 1 sc, 1 sc in next sc, 3 sc in 1 sc, 1 sc in each of next 4 sc—20 sts.

(3) Rnd 3: 3 sc in next sc, 1 sc in each of next 3 sc, 3 sc in next sc, 1 sc in each of next 5 sc, 3 sc in next sc, 1 sc in each of next 3 sc, 3 sc in next sc, 1 sc in each of next 6 sc—28 sts.

(4) Rnd 4, 5, 6: 1 sc in each sc—28 sts.

(5) Rnd 7: 1 sc in each of next 22 sc, sl st in back loop of next sc.

CROCHET THE HANDLE

(6) Ch 18, join to tenth sc from beginning of ch, turn and sl st in last 3 ch, ch 4, join to fourth sc from last handle connection, making a V, turn and sl st in next 3 ch of last ch 4, sl st in each ch of handle to last 3 ch, ch 4, join to fourth sc before beginning of handle, turn and sl st along each ch 4 of V; fasten off.

(7) Cut fabric and weave ends into basket with large needle or smaller hook.

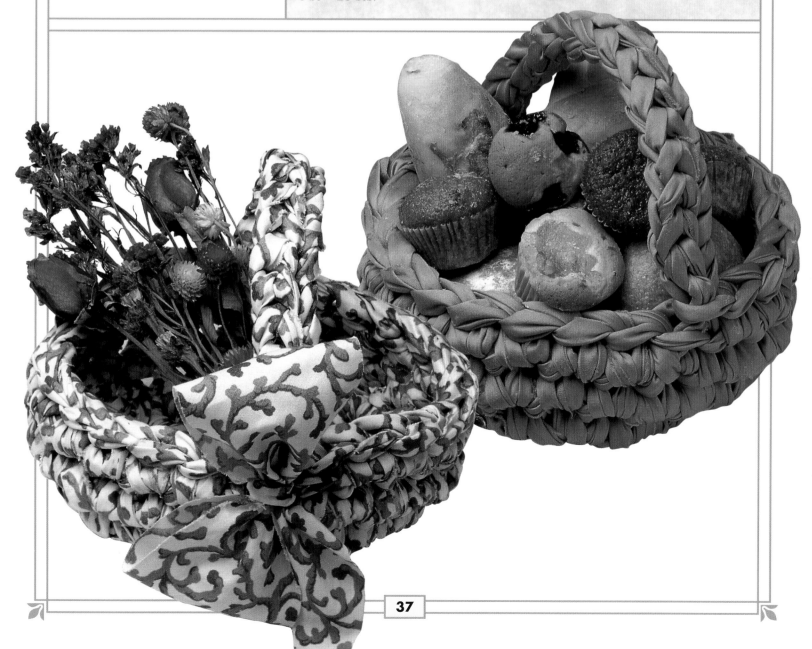

Hoppy Housekeepers

Larger-than-life bunnies are happy to lend a hand with the housework! Sew fuzzy friends from soft, fluffy felt or plush felt, then dress them in ruffled dresses and aprons made from cotton fabric to match your kitchen or laundry room. One bunny sits happily atop a vacuum cleaner, while the other joins the cleanup brigade by offering paper towels.

Vacuum Cover

YOU WILL NEED

- Gallon plastic milk jug
- 1½ yds (1.4m) of pink plush felt
- Sewing machine with zigzag stitch
- 1 yd (91.5cm) of gray plush felt
- Polyester fiberfill
- 12" × 21" (30.5 × 53.5cm) piece of white plush felt
- Pink sewing thread
- 1" (2.5cm) square of ivory felt, for teeth
- ¾" (2cm) buttons: 2 blue round and 1 pink heart-shaped
- ½ yd (45.5cm) of floral striped fabric
- 2½ yds (2.3m) of plaid fabric
- 2 yds (1.8m) of blue cotton fabric
- 3⅛ yds (2.9m) of print fabric
- 7½" × 32" (19 × 81cm) piece of lightweight fusible interfacing

CUT AND COVER THE JUG

① Cut off the bottom of the jug with the craft knife.

② Cut a 14" × 24" (35.5 × 61cm) piece of pink plush felt. Wrap and glue the plush felt around the sides of the jug, letting the plush felt extend evenly at the top and bottom of the jug. Smooth the plush felt over the curves, gluing as you go. Tuck and glue the excess plush felt into the jug opening at the top, and over the cut edges at the bottom.

MAKE THE HEAD

③ Cut a 12" × 16" (30.5 × 40.5cm) piece of pink plush felt. Fold it in

CRAFTER'S TIP

All seam allowances are ½" (1.5cm) unless otherwise noted.

half crosswise with right sides together. Place the head pattern on the center of the folded plush felt. Draw around the outline of the pattern with a disappearing-ink marker.

④ Pin fabric layers together. Sew along the marked line, leaving a 3" (7.5cm) opening along the bottom of the head. Cut away the excess fabric ½" (1.5cm) outside the stitching or marked line. Clip the seam allowances along the curves. Turn the head right side out, and stuff with fiberfill. Turn under ½" (1.5cm) on the opening edge, and slip stitch the opening closed.

⑤ Cut an 8" × 11" (20.5 × 28cm) piece of white plush felt. Fold in half lengthwise with right sides together. Place the muzzle pattern on the center of the folded plush felt. Draw around the outline of the pattern with a disappearing marker. Pin the fabric layers together. Sew along the marked line. Cut away the extra fabric ½" (1.5cm) outside the stitching. Clip the seam allowances along the curves. Cut a 2" (5cm) slit in one layer of the muzzle. Turn right side out through the slit. Stuff lightly with fiberfill, and slip stitch the opening closed.

⑥ Using the muzzle pattern as a guide, draw the mouth on the muzzle front. Stitch over the markings through all layers, using a machine satin stitch and pink thread. Place the teeth pattern on the ivory felt. Draw around the outline of the pattern with a disappearing marker.

⑦ Using the teeth pattern as a guide, outline each tooth with the black marker. Glue the teeth just below the smile.

⑧ Glue the heart button above the smile for a nose. Glue the muzzle onto the front of the head, near the lower edge. Sew the round buttons onto the head for eyes, placing them just above the muzzle.

⑨ Cut a 10" × 12" (25.5 × 30.5cm) piece each of white and pink plush felt. Place the pieces with right sides together and edges even. Place the ear pattern near one edge of the layered plush felt, leaving a ½" (1.5cm) border around all the pattern edges. Draw around the outline of the pattern with a disappearing marker. Move the pattern, and place it near the other edge of the plush felt to mark another ear.

⑩ Pin the fabric layers together. Sew along the marked lines, leaving the short, straight edge open on

each ear. Cut the extra fabric ½" (1.5cm) away from each stitching or marking line. Clip the seam allowances along the curves. Turn each ear right side out. Turn under ½" (1.5cm) on the opening edge, and slip stitch the opening shut. Topstitch each ear ¼" (6mm) from the curved edges.

11 Glue the ears behind the head so that the straight edges of the ears cross at the bottom.

12 Glue the head on the jug, placing the jug handle in back.

MAKE THE ARMS

13 To make the arms, cut a 14" × 26" (35.5 × 66cm) piece of pink plush felt, and fold it in half crosswise with right sides together. Place the vacuum cover arm pattern near one edge of the folded plush felt, leaving a ½" (1.5cm) border around all the pattern edges. Draw around the outline of the pattern with disappearing-ink fabric marker. Move the pattern and place it near the other edge of the plush felt to mark the other arm.

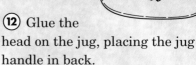

14 Pin the fabric layers together. Sew along the marked lines, leaving the short, straight edge open on each arm. Cut away the extra fabric ½" (1.5cm) from each stitching or marking line. Clip the seam allowances along the curves. Turn each arm right side out. Stuff with fiberfill. Turn under ½" (1.5cm) on the opening edge, and slip stitch the

opening shut. Glue the arms on the back of the jug, just below the head.

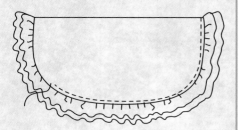

MAKE THE APRON

15 To make the apron, fold the floral striped fabric in half crosswise. Cut one lower corner in a curve through both layers for the apron hem. Unfold the fabric.

16 Fold one corner of the plaid fabric to mark the bias grain. Cut along the fold. Keep the triangle to make the bow.

17 Cut three 4" (10cm) wide strips from the remaining plaid. Sew the strips end to end, with right sides together, with ½" (1.5cm) seams. Cut a 120" (205cm) piece from the strip for the ruffle.

18 Fold the ruffle in half lengthwise, with wrong sides together. To gather the ruffle, sew long machine stitches ¼" (6mm) and ½" (1.5cm) from the long raw edges, but do not cut the thread. Pull threads to gather. Pin the ruffle to the right side of the apron hem, keeping the raw edges even.

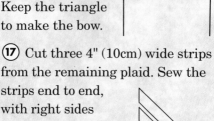

19 In the same way, make a 5" (13cm) wide ruffle from the blue fabric. Pin the blue ruffle over the plaid ruffle, keeping the raw edges even. Sew the ruffles to the apron through all layers. Press the seam allowances toward the apron. Topstitch the apron ¼" (6mm) from the ruffle seam.

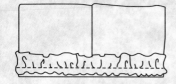

MAKE THE SKIRT

20 Cut the following pieces across the width of the print fabric: two 36" (91.5cm) skirts and two 36" (91.5cm) waistbands. Cut a 25" (63.5cm) square of print fabric for the shawl. Sew the skirt pieces, right sides together, along one short edge for a side seam.

21 Make a 6" (15cm) wide blue ruffle the same as for the apron, but make this ruffle 180" (357.5cm) long for the hem of the skirt. Sew the ruffle to the right side of the skirt hem, keeping the raw edges even. Press the seam allowances toward the skirt.

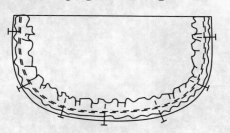

22 Sew the remaining side seam of the skirt, continuing to sew the ruffle together. Cut a 7" (18cm) slit in the center back of the skirt, at the waist edge. Turn under ¼" (6mm) on the edges of the slit, and edge stitch.

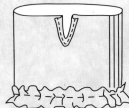

23 To gather the skirt and apron, sew long machine stitches ¼" (6mm) and ½" (1.5cm) from the waist edge of each piece. Do not cut the thread. Pull up the threads to gather the skirt to 22" (56cm). Pull up the threads to gather the apron to 19" (48cm). Knot the thread ends to secure the gathers. Pin the apron to the skirt, right sides up, with raw edges even. The skirt will extend 1½" (4cm) past the apron at each end.

24 Sew the waistband pieces in a ½" (1.5cm) seam, right sides together, along one short edge for the center seam. Fold the waistband in half lengthwise with right sides together. Sew the long edges together, leaving a 22" (56cm) opening in the center. Sew each short end diagonally. Trim away the extra fabric. Clip the seam allowances at each end of the stitching.

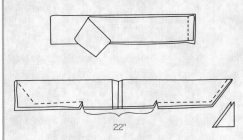

22"

25 Pin the apron and skirt to one layer of the waistband between clips, right sides together. Keep the other layer of the waistband free as you sew the apron and skirt to the waistband in a ½" (1.5cm) seam.

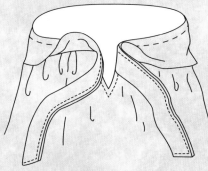

26 Turn the waistband right side out, continuing to turn under the unstitched waistband edge. Edge stitch the waistband through all layers above the skirt.

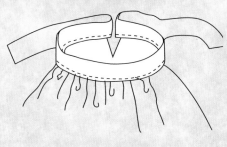

ASSEMBLE

27 Place the skirt on the jug just below the arms, with the opening in the back. Tie the long ends of the waistband into a bow. Make a 3½" (9cm) wide plaid ruffle the same as for the apron, but make this ruffle 95" (241cm) long for the shawl. Pull up the threads to gather the ruffle. Baste the ruffle along 2 edges of the right side of the shawl, keeping the raw edges even. Taper the ends of the ruffle at the shawl corners.

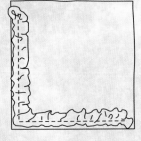

28 Fold the shawl in half diagonally, with right sides together. Sew the edges together, leaving a 3" (7.5cm) opening along one edge. Turn right side out through the opening. Tie the shawl around the neck.

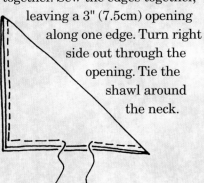

MAKE A BOW

29 Cut a 7½" × 32" (19 × 81cm) bias piece of plaid fabric from the reserved triangle for the bow. Follow the interfacing manufacturer's instructions to fuse the interfacing onto the wrong side of the bow. Sew the short ends of the bow together. Press the seam open in the center of the bow.

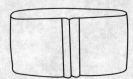

30 Sew the long edges of the bow together, leaving a 3" (7.5cm) opening in the center of one edge. Turn right side out through the opening.

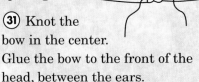

31 Knot the bow in the center. Glue the bow to the front of the head, between the ears.

DRESS THE VACUUM

32 Lift the bunny by the back of the head (the jug handle) and slip the jug over the vacuum cleaner handle. Arrange the skirt to cover the vacuum.

Paper Towel Holder

YOU WILL NEED

- Folding paper towel holder with screws

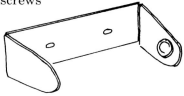

- 11" × 14" (28 × 35.5cm) piece of heavy cardboard
- 5" × 12" (13 × 30.5cm) piece of ¼" (6mm) foam board
- 1 yd (1m) gray plush felt
- Polyester fiberfill
- 1" (2.5cm) square of ivory felt, for teeth
- ¾" (2cm) buttons: 2 blue round and 1 pink heart-shaped
- 2 wing nuts to fit screws of paper towel holder
- ½ yd (45.5m) of floral striped fabric
- 12" × 21" (30.5 × 53cm) piece of white plush felt
- 2½ yds (2.3m) of plaid fabric
- 2 yds (1.8m) of blue cotton fabric
- 6" × 23" (15 × 58.5cm) piece of print fabric
- 7½" × 32" (19 × 81cm) piece of lightweight fusible interfacing
- 8" (20.5cm) of heavy picture wire

MAKE THE HOLDER

① Center the paper towel holder along one short side of the cardboard. Mark the position of the screw holes on the board. Set the towel holder aside. Use the point of the craft knife to pierce holes in the cardboard at the marks.

② Draw a line across the foam board, 7" (18cm) below the short end, to mark the neck. Cut a 7" × 11" (18 × 28cm) piece of gray plush felt. Wrap and glue the plush felt around the board above the neck mark, overlapping the ends of the center back.

MAKE THE BUNNY

③ To make the head, see the directions for the Vacuum Cover using gray plush felt. Cut a 5" (13cm) long slit in the back of the head, 2" (5cm) above the lower edge. Insert the covered end of the foam board into the slit so that 2" (5cm) of plush felt shows below the head. Glue the slit edge of the plush felt onto the board.

④ To make the arms, see the directions for the Vacuum Cover using gray plush felt. Use the towel holder arm pattern. Stuff the fingers lightly with fiberfill. Slide a bunny arm onto each arm of the towel holder.

⑤ Use a craft knife to cut a hole in each paw to allow the paper-holding knob to protrude. Stuff the bunny arm through the upper edge and hole. Arrange the stuffing so that it is on the outside of the towel holder. Glue the plush felt around the edge of the knob. Glue the upper arms to the holder.

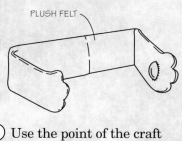

PLUSH FELT

⑥ Use the point of the craft knife to pierce the plush felt over the screw holes. Insert screws through the holes on the holder and cardboard, and tighten a wing nut on each screw to hold the towel holder firmly to the cardboard.

⑦ Glue the uncovered end of the foam board behind the cardboard.

⑧ To make the apron, see the directions for the Vacuum Cover. Gather the apron to 22" (56cm). Knot the thread ends to secure the gathers.

⑨ Press under ½" (1.5cm) on one long edge of the print fabric for the waistband.

10 Sew the apron to the unpressed edge of the waistband in a ½" (1.5cm) seam, right sides together and raw edges even. The waistband will extend ½" (1.5cm) past the apron at each end.

11 Fold the waistband in half lengthwise with right sides together. Sew across the short ends.

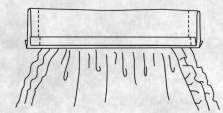

12 Turn the waistband right side out. Topstitch the waistband through all layers. Glue the waistband around the board, with the ends at center back.

13 To make a bow, see the directions for the Vacuum Cover.

14 Twist a wire end around each wing nut to form a hanging loop.

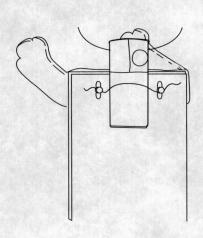

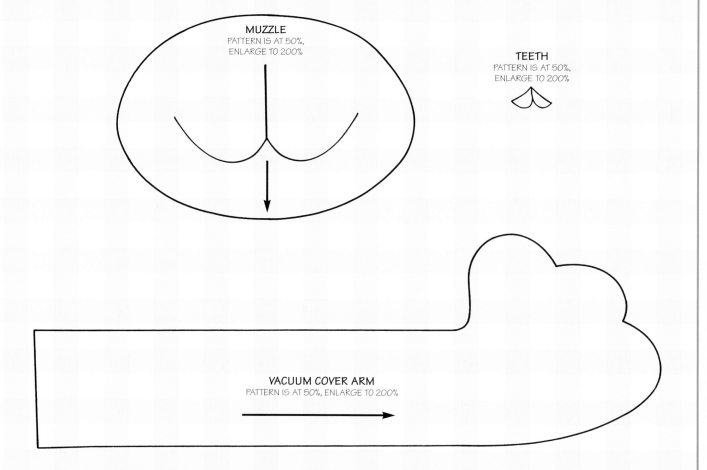

MUZZLE
PATTERN IS AT 50%,
ENLARGE TO 200%

TEETH
PATTERN IS AT 50%,
ENLARGE TO 200%

VACUUM COVER ARM
PATTERN IS AT 50%, ENLARGE TO 200%

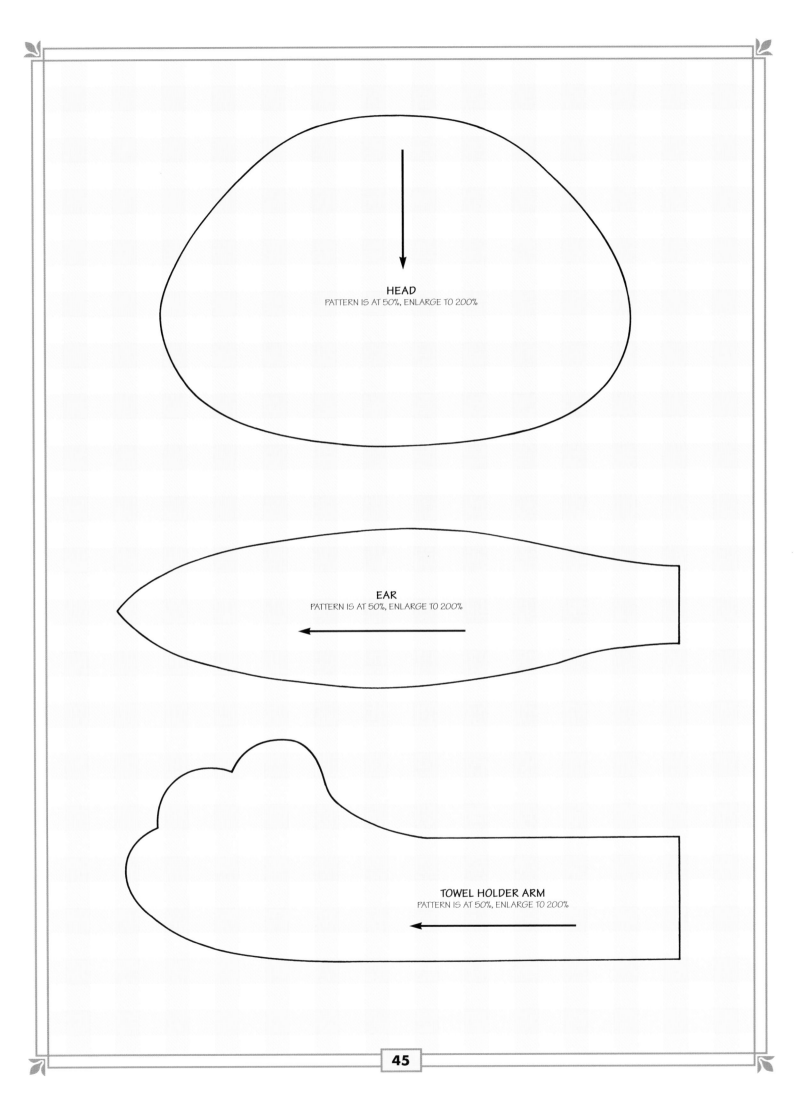

HEAD
PATTERN IS AT 50%, ENLARGE TO 200%

EAR
PATTERN IS AT 50%, ENLARGE TO 200%

TOWEL HOLDER ARM
PATTERN IS AT 50%, ENLARGE TO 200%

Chapter Three

A Country Bedroom

Posie Pillows

Beautiful fabric roses adorn these two pillows, perfect for a romantic country bedroom. They're easy accents you can craft without any sewing!

Love Letter Pillow

YOU WILL NEED

- ⅜ yd (34.5cm) each of 4 assorted floral print fabrics
- 34-gauge beading wire
- Lightweight cardboard covered with aluminum foil
- Standard-size pastel yellow pillowcase
- ⅝ yd (57cm) of paper-backed fusible web, 18" (45.5cm) wide
- 5" × 11" (13 × 28cm) piece of white fabric
- 2" (5cm) square of red fabric
- 3½" × 7" (9 × 18cm) piece of light green fabric
- 3½" × 10" (9 × 25.5cm) piece of dark green fabric
- 3 yds (2.7m) of green satin ribbon, ¼" (6mm) wide
- Standard-size bed pillow
- Fusible hem tape, ¾" (2cm) wide
- 1½ yds (1.4m) of purple ribbon, 1" (2.5cm) wide
- Large safety pin

MAKE ROSES

① To make 7 large, 4 medium, and 3 small roses from floral print fabrics, cut one fabric strip for each rose.

ROSE	CUT FABRIC STRIP
LARGE	3½" × 24" (9 × 61cm)
MEDIUM	2½" × 24" (6.5 × 61cm)
SMALL	2½" × 12" (6.5 × 30.5cm)

② Cut a piece of beading wire 4" (5cm) longer than each fabric strip. Turn under ½" (1.5cm) on the long edges of each fabric strip. Press.

③ Open one folded edge of each fabric strip to lay wire along the fold. Tape one end of the wire to the work surface to keep the wire from shifting. Fold the raw edge over the wire, and glue in place. Encase the wire with fabric, but do not glue the wire to the fabric.

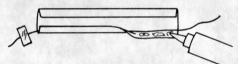

④ Fold each strip in half. Glue the long edges together.

⑤ Gather each fabric strip tightly by sliding it on the wire. Fold one corner of the strip down. Roll the gathered fabric around the folded corner, applying glue to the lower edge every half turn. Twist the wire ends together.

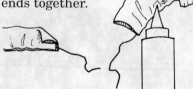

CRAFTER'S TIP

Select standard-size pillowcases in solid pastel colors to make these pretty pillows. For the appliqués and fabric roses, choose lightweight fabrics such as cotton blend broadcloth, sheeting, or soft satin.

6 Place aluminum foil–covered cardboard inside the pillowcase to prevent glue from seeping through. Use silicone glue to glue each rose to the pillowcase. Let the glue dry.

MAKE APPLIQUÉS

7 To make the appliqués, trace the patterns onto the smooth side of paper-backed fusible web. Trace the envelope and the heart patterns once each. Trace the leaf pattern ten times.

8 Cut out each motif pattern with a generous margin of web all around the traced outline. Place the envelope pattern with the web rough side down to the wrong side of blue fabric and fuse. In the same way, apply the heart to the red fabric, four leaves to light green fabric and six leaves to dark green fabric.

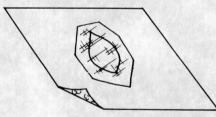

9 Cut out each appliqué motif along the traced pattern outline. Do not remove the paper backing until you are ready to fuse each appliqué in place.

MAKE A PILLOW

10 To prepare the pillowcase, cut off the finished hem from the pillowcase. Turn under the raw edge ¾" (2cm). Press.

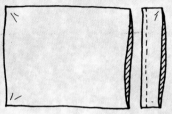

11 Mark the center of the pillowcase with pins. Use a disappearing marker to draw a placement line about 4" (10cm) long diagonally through the center.

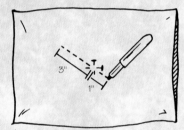

12 For stems, cut 8"–10" (20–25.5cm) pieces of ¼" (6mm) wide ribbon. Slip aluminum foil-covered cardboard inside the pillowcase. Glue one end of each ribbon at the lower end of the diagonal placement line. Fold the envelope appliqué on the fold lines. Peel off the paper backing and fuse. Apply paper-backed fusible web to the back of the envelope.

13 Position the envelope flap side up on an angle near the ribbon stems. Peel off the paper backing to fuse in place. Peel off the paper backing to fuse the heart to the envelope flap.

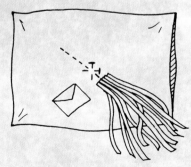

14 Arrange 3 large roses over the glued ends of the ribbon stems, and pin. Arrange the remaining roses in a bouquet with the smaller roses at the top of the diagonal placement line, and pin. Arrange the leaves around the roses. Peel off the paper backings to fuse the leaves in place. Remove the pins as you glue each rose in place. Let the glue dry.

15 To finish the pillow, insert a standard-size bed pillow into the decorated pillowcase. Close the open end of the pillowcase with fusible hem tape.

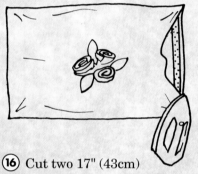

16 Cut two 17" (43cm) pieces of 1" (2.5cm) wide ribbon to make a double bow. Overlap ends of each ribbon to make a loop. With the lapped ends face down, tie the loops in the center with the remaining piece of ribbon. Use a safety pin to attach the bow to the pillowcase at the base of the bouquet.

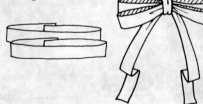

Basket of Roses Pillow

YOU WILL NEED

- ⅜ yd (.4m) each of 4 assorted floral print fabrics
- 34-gauge beading wire
- ⅝ yd (57cm) of paper-backed fusible web, 18" (45cm) wide
- 7" × 11" (18 × 28cm) piece each of light green and brown fabric
- 4" × 20" (10 × 51cm) piece of dark green fabric
- 4" × 9" (10 × 23cm) piece of medium green fabric
- Standard-sized pastel pink pillowcase
- Lightweight cardboard covered with aluminum foil
- Clear silicone fabric glue
- Standard-size bed pillow
- Fusible hem tape, ¾" (2cm) wide

MAKE THE ROSES

① Make the following roses as in Love Letter Pillow: 8 large, 3 medium, and 3 small roses from floral print fabrics.

MAKE APPLIQUÉS

② Make the following appliques as in Love Letter Pillow and using the patterns on page 52: 1 inner basket from light green fabric; 1 outer basket from brown; 5 large leaves from dark green; 2 large leaves from medium green; 3 small leaves from dark green; and 3 small leaves from medium green.

③ Peel off the paper backings to fuse each small dark green leaf to another small green leaf with wrong sides together.

④ Fuse the brown outer basket appliqué to the green inner planter appliqué.

MAKE THE PILLOW

⑤ See Love Letter Pillow to prepare the pillowcase.

⑥ Center the basket appliqué on the pillowcase about 2½" (6.5cm) above the bottom edge. Peel off the paper backing to fuse it in place.

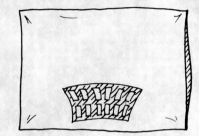

⑦ Arrange the roses around the top of the basket, and pin. Arrange the large leaves around the roses. Remove the paper backings to fuse the large leaves in place.

⑧ Slip aluminum foil–covered cardboard inside the pillow. Glue each rose in place with silicon glue.

⑨ Glue the edge of each small leaf in place among the roses. Let the glue dry.

⑩ Remove foil–covered cardboard. See Love Letter Pillow to finish.

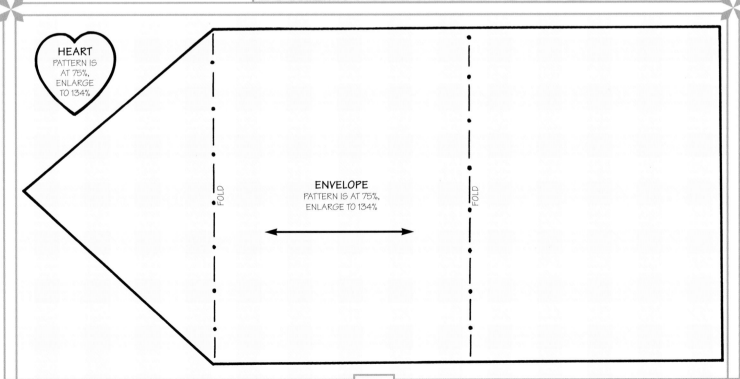

HEART
PATTERN IS AT 75%, ENLARGE TO 134%

FOLD

FOLD

ENVELOPE
PATTERN IS AT 75%, ENLARGE TO 134%

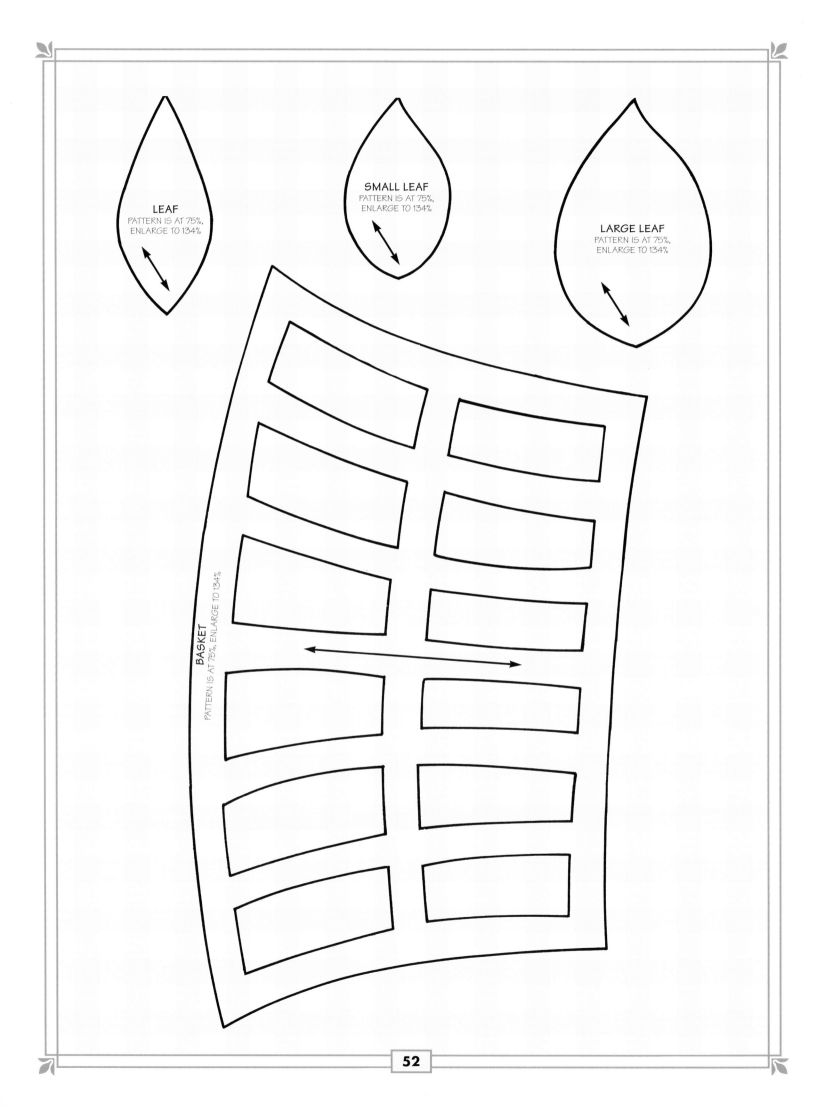

LEAF
PATTERN IS AT 75%,
ENLARGE TO 134%

SMALL LEAF
PATTERN IS AT 75%,
ENLARGE TO 134%

LARGE LEAF
PATTERN IS AT 75%,
ENLARGE TO 134%

BASKET
PATTERN IS AT 75%, ENLARGE TO 134%

Easy Ruffled Baskets

Ruffled baskets made with pretty prints are useful in any room of the house. Ours are made for just pennies by using a small bucket or a plastic soda bottle for the base. The big basket is perfect for a flowerpot coverup or for guest hand towels. The smaller basket is useful for buttons and pins, a small plant, keys, coins, or even wrapped candies. Thrifty and quick to sew, either basket can be crafted in an hour or less.

Big Floral Basket

YOU WILL NEED

- ⅜ yd (34.5cm) of leaf print fabric
- ⅝ yd (57cm) of floral print fabric
- ½ yd (45.5cm) of batting
- Heavy cardboard
- 2½ quart (2.5l) cardboard bucket
- ⅞" × 15" (2cm × 38cm) strip of poster board
- Bodkin or safety pin
- 24" (61cm) of elastic, ¼" (6mm) wide
- ¾ yd (68.5cm) of ribbon, ⅝" (1.5cm) wide
- 1⅛ yds (1m) of ribbon, ¼" (6mm) wide
- 3 silk roses
- Compass with pencil

CUT THE FABRIC

① Cut from leaf print fabric: a 10" × 25" (25.5 × 63.5cm) basket lining and the 6½" (16.5cm) circle for the base lining. Cut from floral print fabric: a 12" × 45" (30.5 × 114cm) cover, a 2½" × 32" (6.5 × 81cm) handle and the 6½" (16.5cm) circle for the cover bottom. Cut from batting: two 5" × 24" (13 × 61cm) strips, the 6½" (16.5cm) circle twice, and the 5½" (14cm) circle twice. Cut the 5½" (14cm) circle from cardboard for a base. Patterns are on page 56.

MAKE THE BASKET

② To make a gathered lining, sew the short ends of the basket lining in a ¼" (6mm) seam with right sides together. Sew long stitches ⅜" (1cm) and ½" (1.5cm) from the bottom edge.

③ Pull the threads to gather the lining to fit the inside bottom of the container. Tie the threads in a knot, and trim off the thread tails. Glue the gathered part of the lining to the inside of the container. Fold the raw edge of the lining over the top edge of the container and glue.

④ Glue two batting circles to the cardboard base. Center the base lining right side up over the batting.

(5) Fold the lining over the edge of the cardboard base and glue.

(6) Insert the base, fabric side up, into the container and glue.

(7) Sew the long edges of the handle in a ¼" (6mm) seam with right sides together. Turn right side out.

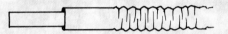

(8) Thread the poster board strip through the handle, shirring it to fit. Glue the shirred fabric to each end of the handle, then glue or hand stitch each end of the handle to the outside of the container.

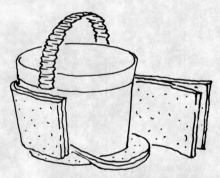

(9) Glue two batting circles to the bottom of the container. Glue the batting strips around the outside of the container.

(10) Sew the short ends of the cover in a ¼" (6mm) seam with right sides together. Turn under the top raw edge ¼" (6mm), then 2½" (6.5cm). Stitch close to the lower fold, leaving a 1" (2.5cm) opening. Sew another row of stitches ⅜" (1cm) above the first to form a casing.

LEAVE OPEN

(11) Sew long stitches ⅜" (1cm) and ½" (1.5cm) from the bottom edge of the cover.

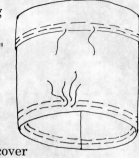

(12) Pin the cover bottom to the cover with right sides together. Pull the threads to gather the cover to fit the bottom. Sew a ¼" (6mm) seam.

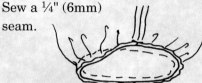

(13) Use a bodkin or safety pin to thread elastic through the casing. Lap the ends of the elastic and sew them together. Pull the threads to gather the cover to fit the bottom. Sew a ¼" (6mm) seam.

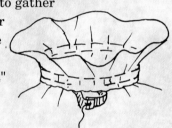

(14) Sew the opening closed. Turn the cover right side out. Put the cover on the container.

MAKE A BOW

(15) Fold the ⅝" (1.5cm) wide ribbon into two loops and the ¼" (6mm) wide ribbon into three loops. Tie each group of loops in the center with thread to make a bow. Trim the ribbon ends in a V.

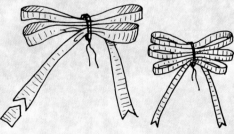

(16) Glue the bow to the center front of the basket, over the casing. Glue roses over the bow.

Button Basket

YOU WILL NEED

- ½ yd (45.5m) each of 2 print fabrics
- Heavy cardboard
- ¼ yd (23cm) of batting
- 2 liter soda bottle
- 1" × 14" (2.5 × 35.5cm) strip of poster board
- 1¾ yds (1.6m) of medium rickrack
- 1 yd (91.5cm) of baby rickrack
- 12 assorted buttons

CUT THE FABRIC

(1) Cut a 7½" × 14½" (19 × 37cm) basket lining and the 5½" (14cm) circle for a base lining from one fabric. Cut a 2½" × 14" (6.5 × 35.5cm) handle from the other fabric. Cut a 14½" (37cm) square from each fabric. Fold each square into quarters to cut the 14½" (37cm) circle for the cover and cover lining. Cut the 3½" (9cm) circle once from cardboard for the base, and twice from batting. Cut the 9" (23cm) circle twice from batting.

MAKE THE BASKET

(2) Trim the bottle to 3" (7.5cm) tall.

(3) Make a gathered lining following the directions for the Big Floral Basket.

④ Fold the handle in half with right sides together. Sew the long edges in a ¼" (6mm) seam, leaving the short ends open. Turn right side out. Thread the poster board strip into the handle.

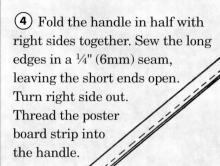

⑤ Glue the ends of the handle to the outside of the bottle.

⑥ To make a lined cover, cut a 1½" (4cm) slit in the lining.

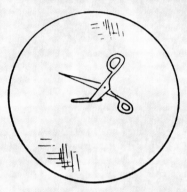

⑦ Sew the cover and lining in a ¼" (6mm) seam with right sides together.

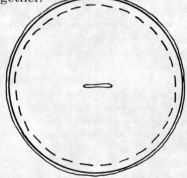

⑧ Clip the seam allowances. Turn the cover right side out through the slit. Sew the slit closed by hand.

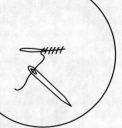

9 Sew long stitches 1¾" (4.5cm) and 2" (5cm) from the edge of the cover.

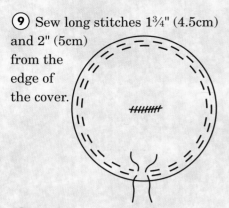

10 Sew medium rickrack around the edge of the cover.

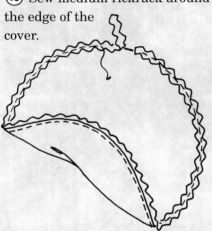

11 Center two batting circles on the cover lining. Place the container on top of the batting.

12 Pull up the threads to gather the cover to fit the container. Tie the threads in a knot, and trim the thread tails.

13 Wrap remaining medium rickrack around the cover, over the gathers. Lap the ends and glue.

MAKE BOWS

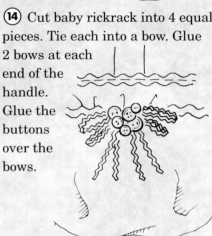

14 Cut baby rickrack into 4 equal pieces. Tie each into a bow. Glue 2 bows at each end of the handle. Glue the buttons over the bows.

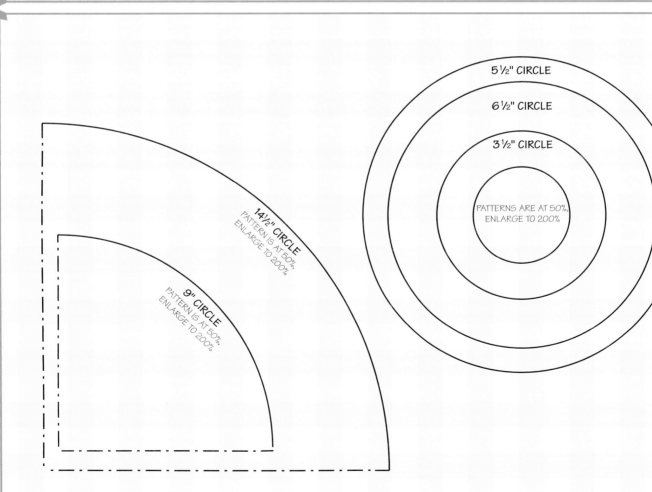

5½" CIRCLE

6½" CIRCLE

3½" CIRCLE

PATTERNS ARE AT 50%, ENLARGE TO 200%

14½" CIRCLE
PATTERN IS AT 50%, ENLARGE TO 200%

9" CIRCLE
PATTERN IS AT 50%, ENLARGE TO 200%

Pretty Pot Coverups

Use these pretty flowerpot covers to dress up cuttings from your garden or everyday houseplants for special housewarming and hostess gifts. Shape cotton fabrics over recycled plastic containers, then trim with ribbons, lace, and rickrack.

Gingham and Lace Pot

YOU WILL NEED

- 1 quart plastic bleach bottle
- 18½" (47cm) square of gingham fabric
- Liquid fabric stiffener
- Elastic cord
- 1⅞ yds (1.7m) of Battenburg lace edging, 1¾" (4.5cm) wide
- 1¼ yds (1.1m) each of 2 colors of ribbon, ¼" (6mm) wide
- 2 silk pansy sprays

CRAFTER'S TIP

Avoid getting finished coverups wet. Remove plants to water them, then replace them in the coverups when dry. If a coverup accidentally gets wet, reshape and let dry.

PREPARE THE PLANTER

① Use a pencil to mark a cutting line on the plastic container 3" (7.5cm) from the bottom. Use old scissors to cut the container.

② Roll a sheet of poster board into a tall tube, and insert it into the bottle so that it fits snugly. Tape the poster board edges together.

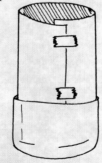

③ Remove the poster board tube from the bottle. Wrap the tube with waxed paper, taping the edges and tucking in the ends.

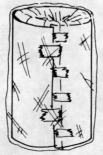

④ Place the wrapped tube into the bottle to complete the form. Turn the form upside down and place it on a large piece of waxed paper.

CUT THE FABRIC

⑤ Fold the fabric in quarters. Cut the raw edges in a curve from corner to corner.

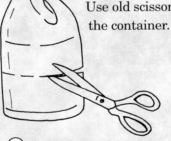

⑥ Glue lace around the circle on the wrong side, overlapping the edges ½" (1.5cm). Let the glue dry.

DRAPE THE FABRIC

⑦ Fold the fabric in quarters to find the center. Mark the center with a small pencil dot on the right side.

57

8 Cover the work surface with waxed paper. Place the fabric right side up on top. Brush liquid fabric stiffener liberally on the fabric.

9 Place the fabric, right side out, over the form. Match the center of the fabric to the center of the bottle. Smooth the fabric down the sides of the form. Tie a piece of elastic cord tightly around the form, 3½" (9cm) from the base. Arrange the fabric folds in soft, even gathers below the cord. Let the fabric dry about 1 hour or until tacky.

SHAPE THE COVERUP

10 Turn the fabric-covered form right side up. Place it on waxed paper. Shape the edges of the coverup with your hands.

11 Let the coverup dry completely overnight. Cut the elastic cord to remove it. Remove the poster board tube but leave the bottle in place.

FINISHING TOUCHES

12 Hold the ribbons together to tie a bow around the coverup, over the gathers. Trim the ribbon ends diagonally.

13 Tuck the pansies into the bow and glue.

Country Rickrack Pot

YOU WILL NEED

- 4" × 4" × 7" (10 × 10 × 18cm) plastic container
- 12" × 15½" (30.5 × 39.5cm) piece of fabric
- 1¾ yds (1.6m) gathered edging, 2" (5cm) wide
- Liquid fabric stiffener
- Elastic cord
- 1½ yds (1.4m) jumbo rickrack

PREPARE THE PLANTER AND CUT THE FABRIC

① See Gingham and Lace Pot on pages 57–58 to prepare the planter. Do not cut the container.

② Fold the fabric into quarters. Cut the raw edges in a curve to make an oval.

③ Sew the gathered edging around the oval on the right side. Overlap the edging ends ½" (1.5cm).

DRAPE AND SHAPE THE CONTAINER

④ See the Gingham and Lace Pot to drape the fabric, tying it below the gathered edging.

⑤ See Gingham and Lace Pot to shape the coverup. Arrange the gathered edging in a soft ruffle.

FINISHING TOUCHES

⑥ Tie rickrack in a bow around the bottom of the gathered edging and glue. Trim the rickrack ends diagonally.

Vintage Yo-Yo Pillow

Yo-yos are dear little circles of fabric, gathered with hand stitches, that were usually sewn together into summer bedspreads, dresser scarves, and pillow shams. This pillow design is a good size for using vintage yo-yo pieces that are still in good condition, perhaps from a large but tattered coverlet. If you don't have old yo-yos, you can stitch new ones from fabric scraps or even reproduction vintage cotton prints.

Each finished yo-yo will be about 2" (5cm) in diameter.

YOU WILL NEED

- Polyester fiberfill
- 11" × 22" (28 × 56cm) piece of solid fabric
- ⅛ yd (11.5cm) each: 10 assorted print fabrics

CRAFTER'S TIP

The more fabrics in the yo-yo mix, the better, so feel free to substitute fabric in the styles of your choice.

MAKE YO-YOS

① Cut out 49 circles, 4½" (11cm) in diameter from the wrong side of the fabrics.

② Fold under the raw edge of each yo-yo ¼" (6mm). Sew long running stitches along the fold.

③ Pull the thread to gather the circle closed. Secure the gathers with a few, small stitches. Smooth and flatten each yo-yo.

MAKE THE PILLOW

④ Cut the solid fabric into two 11" (28cm) squares for the pillow front and back. Sew them with right sides together in a ¼" (6mm) seam, leaving a 2" (5cm) opening along one edge. Trim diagonally across the corners. Turn the pillow right side out.

⑤ Stuff the pillow firmly with fiberfill, using a blunt stuffing tool to reach the corners. Sew the opening closed with small hand stitches.

COVER PILLOW

⑥ Arrange the yo-yos in 7 rows of 7 each to make the pillow overlay.

⑦ Use a few small stitches to join the yo-yos at their edges. Sew from the wrong side.

⑧ Center the overlay, right side up, over the pillow front so that a row of yo-yos extends all around. Sew the inner edges of the outer yo-yos to the seams of pillow.

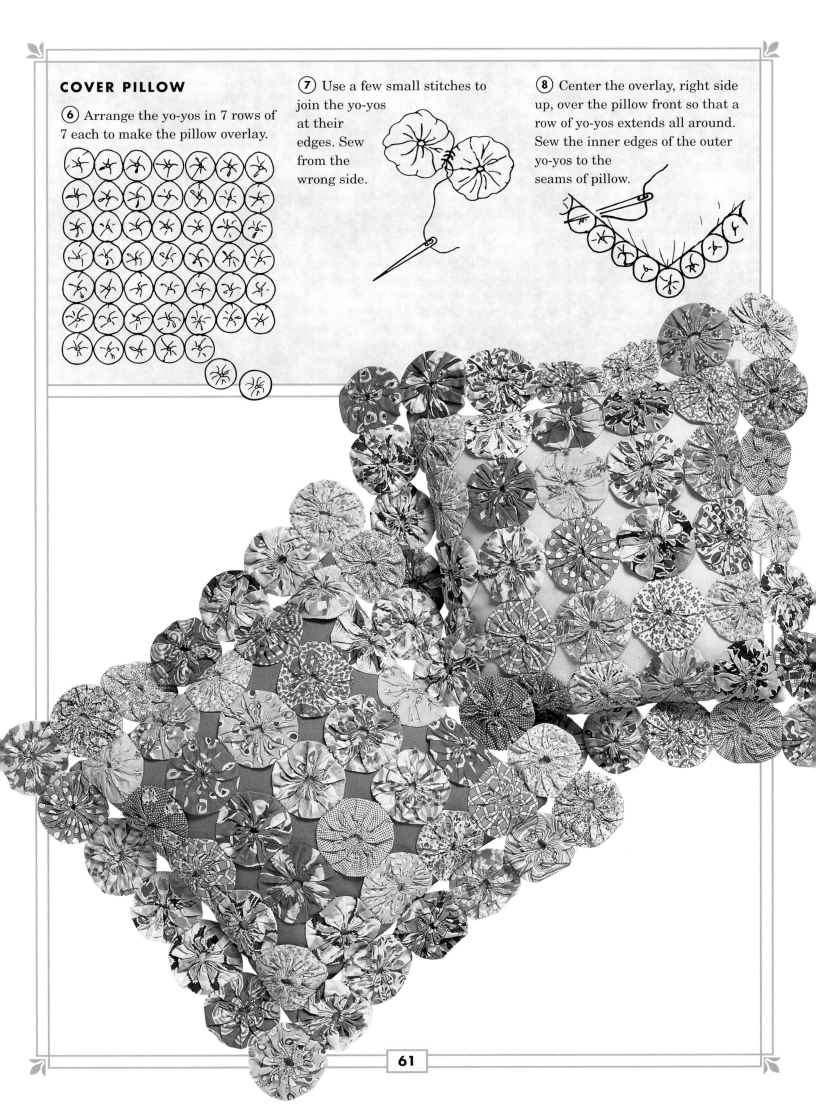

61

Hearts and Flowers Garland

A graceful garland can add a touch of country to a framed picture or mirror. It's perfect hanging below a shelf or topping a window. Ribbons add romance to the grapevine twigs, and little cottage roses and tiny hummingbirds help to bring the garden indoors.

YOU WILL NEED

- 3 heart-shaped grapevine wreaths, 4" (10cm)
- 6 round grapewine wreaths, 3" (7.5cm)
- 5 yds of satin ribbon, ⅛" (3mm) wide
- 3 yds of satin ribbon, ⅜" (1cm) wide, in each of 2 colors
- About 6 bunches of silk flowers with leaves
- 5 silk roses, 1½" (3.8cm)
- 12 silk rosebuds, 1" (2.5cm)
- 9 small berry sprigs
- 3 craft hummingbirds, approximately 3" (7.5cm) long
- 28-gauge spool wire

CRAFTER'S TIP

Choose flowers and ribbon in colors to match your home decor!

MAKE A GARLAND

① Using the spool wire, join the grapevine wreaths together at the side of each wreath. Begin with two round wreaths, then each heart alternating with a round wreath and end with the two remaining round wreaths.

② Cut four 18" pieces of ⅛" (3mm) wide ribbon. Wrap a piece around each of the four round wreaths in the middle of the garland. Glue the ribbon ends in back.

③ To make four tassels, cut the remaining ⅛" (3mm) wide ribbon into eight equal lengths, about 11" (28cm) each. For each tassel, hold two pieces of ribbon together and fold in half. Wrap wire around the ribbon near the fold. Glue a ribbon tassel to the bottom of each of the four ribbon-wrapped wreaths. Cut ribbon ends diagonally.

④ Cut from each color of ⅜" (1cm) wide ribbon: three 18" (45.5cm) pieces. Fold a 3" (7.5cm) loop at one ribbon end. Hold three loops of each color together and wrap wire around to make a bow. Glue a bow behind each end wreath. Cut ribbon ends diagonally.

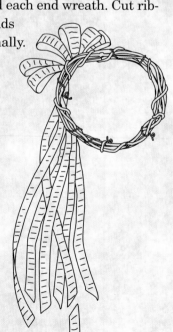

⑤ Cut apart the bunches of silk flowers and trim away the stems. Glue the flowers along the upper and lower curves of each wreath. Glue a silk rose on each heart and end wreath. Glue one or two rosebuds, berry sprigs and silk leaves to each wreath. Glue hummingbirds to the garland.

MAKE A HANGING LOOP

⑥ Cut two 10" (25.5cm) pieces of wire. Fold each wire in half and twist.

⑦ Fold the twisted wire in half, and twist the strands together to form a 1" (2.5cm) loop.

⑧ Twist the ends of a hanging loop around the vines at each end of the garland.

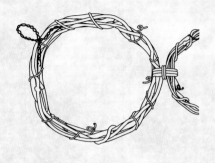

Chapter Four

A Touch of Country Throughout the House

Country Couple

Create this cute country couple for your door or wall from a decorative craft broom and some fabric and ribbon!

YOU WILL NEED

- 32" (81cm) straw craft broom
- Serrated knife
- 30-gauge spool wire
- 7" × 14" (18 × 35.5cm) piece of muslin, for heads
- 7" × 14" (18 × 35.5cm) piece of lightweight polyester batting, for heads
- 2" (5cm) Styrofoam ball
- 3" × 14" (7.5 × 35.5cm) piece of lightweight cardboard
- 8 yds (7.5m) of yellow chenille yarn, for hair
- 12" (30.5cm) of red woven-edge satin ribbon, ⅛" (3mm) wide
- Two 4" (10cm) diameter straw hats
- Rubber band
- ¼ yd (23cm) of yellow plaid fabric for his sleeves

- 23" (58.5cm) of light brown paper twist ribbon, for arms
- ⅓ yd (.3m) of green gingham farm-print fabric, for his pants
- 18" (45.5cm) length of raffia
- ⅓ yd (30.5cm) of red gingham farm-print fabric for her sleeves and skirt
- 23" (58.5cm) of white lace, 1½" (4cm) wide
- 6 toothpicks
- Small amount of dried mini peppers, bay leaves, and herb sprigs
- 3" (7.5cm) basket
- 3 yds (2.7m) of cow-print ribbon, 2" (5cm) wide
- 2½ yds (2.3m) of red gingham ribbon or fabric strips, 1½" (4cm) wide

② Divide broom bristles in half up the center. To keep them separated, wedge pieces of straw from the cut-off handle into the center between the two sections.

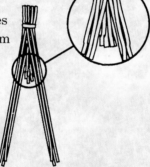

③ Divide the right half of the bristles into 2 equal parts for the farmer's legs. Wrap a 6"–8" (15–20cm) piece of spool wire 2" (5cm) from the bristle bottom to secure each leg section.

DIVIDE THE BROOM

① To divide the broom, use a serrated knife to cut off the broom handle top just above the second handle wrapping. Make a 13" (33cm) long handle with 12"–14" (30.5–35.5cm) long bristles. Set aside the cut-off pieces to use later. Your broom should now have only one handle wrapping at the top. Use the serrated knife or wire cutters to remove any other handle wrapping as shown.

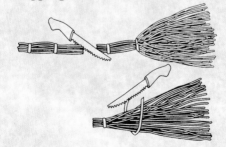

MAKE THE HEADS

④ Cut 2 head patterns each from muslin and batting. With right side of fabric facing down, place a batting circle on each fabric circle. With a needle and doubled thread,

make long running stitches ¼"
(6mm) from the edge through both
fabric and batting.

BATTING

FABRIC

⑤ Using serrated knife, cut
Styrofoam ball in half. With the
fabric facing down, center
Styrofoam half-ball, rounded side
down, on a fabric-and-batting
circle. Pull the thread to gather
the circle closed around the
Styrofoam half-ball. Gather the
fabric tightly and knot thread to
secure. Cover the other Styrofoam
half-ball in the
same manner.

⑥ Attach yarn to each head as
follows: cut a 3" × 4" (7.5 × 10cm)
piece of cardboard and wrap yarn
12 times around the 4" (10cm)
side. Using a small piece of yarn,
tie a knot around the strands at
one end.

4"

7 Remove yarn from cardboard and hot glue knot to top of head. Cut yarn loops and trim ends. For wife's long hair, cut a 3" × 10" (7.5 × 25.5cm) piece of cardboard and wrap yarn 20 times around the 10" (25.5cm) side. Tie a knot around the strands at one end, remove from cardboard, and hot glue knot to top of her head. Trim her hair as desired. Cut two 6" (15cm) pieces of ⅛" (3mm) wide ribbon and tie hair into 2 ponytails.

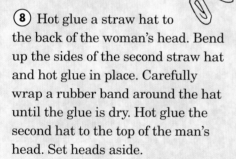

8 Hot glue a straw hat to the back of the woman's head. Bend up the sides of the second straw hat and hot glue in place. Carefully wrap a rubber band around the hat until the glue is dry. Hot glue the second hat to the top of the man's head. Set heads aside.

MAKE SLEEVES AND ARMS

9 Cut a 4½" × 9½" (11.5 × 24cm) piece of sleeve fabric for each doll. Turn under, press, and sew ¼" (6mm) from edge along each 4½" (11.5cm) side. These finished edges will be the sleeve cuffs.

10 Fold each sleeve piece in half lengthwise, right sides together. Sew long side ¼" (6mm) from the edge to make a tube. Turn right side out.

11 To make the arm pieces, cut an 11½" (29cm) piece of paper twist ribbon for each doll. To make hands, fold back ends 1½" (4cm). Wrap a small piece of spool wire around folded ends to hold them in place.

ARM PIECE

12 Slide the paper twist arm piece into the sleeve tube. The hands should show at the cuffs. Wrap about 6" (15cm) of spool wire around each wrist ½" (1.5cm) from the sleeve edge.

13 Starting at the top of the broom bristles, measure about 2" (5cm) up the left handle section. Push your finger into the handle section to separate the straw. Slide the man's covered arms through the handle section as shown. Arms should extend equally on both sides of the handle. Wrap about 12" (30.5cm) of spool wire around the handle section about 2" (5cm) above the arms. Follow the same steps to insert the woman's arms into the other handle section.

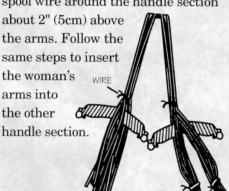

WIRE

MAKE MAN'S PANTS

14 Cut two 9½" × 11½" (24 × 29cm) pieces of pants fabric. Fold both pieces in half crosswise. Use pins to mark the center of each piece. Unfold the fabric.

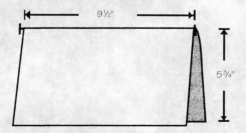

9½"

5¾"

15 Turn under, press, and sew ¼" (6mm) from edge along one 9½" (24cm) side on each piece. These finished edges will be the bottom of the pants legs. With right sides together, place one fabric piece on top of the other. Starting at the top raw edge, sew the pieces together with a ¼" (6mm) seam down both 11½" (29cm) sides, stopping at the pins. Make a small cut in the seam allowance at the end of the stitching, close to but not through the stitches.

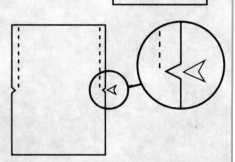

16 Press seams open. Align one seam on top of the other as shown.

17 Starting at the cuff of one leg, sew a ¼" (6mm) seam up to the crotch. Lift presser foot but leave machine needle down in fabric. Rotate the fabric and lower the presser foot to continue sewing down the other leg to the cuff.

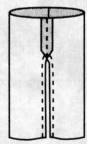

18 Turn the pants right side out. Sew running stitches ½" (1.5cm) from the edge around the waist. With the opening in back, pull pants up over broom bristle "legs." Let 2" (5cm) of bristles stick out at the bottom for feet. Pull threads at top to gather pants to fit waist. Knot thread to keep gathers in place. Hot glue pants waist to broom handle. Wrap the raffia piece around the waist and tie in a bow in back.

MAKE WOMAN'S SKIRT

(19) Cut a 12" × 22" (30.5 × 56cm) piece of skirt fabric. Along one 22" (56cm) edge, turn under ¼" (6mm), press, then sew to make hem. Sew lace to inside of skirt along hem, allowing 1" (2.5cm) of the lace to extend beyond the hem. Next, fold fabric in half crosswise, right sides together. Sew the 12" (30.5cm) sides together ¼" (6mm) from the edge.

(20) With skirt still inside out, make a running stitch ½" (1.5cm) from edge along the skirt top. Slip the skirt, hem first, onto the right-hand broom section as shown below. When the skirt waist is just below the arms, pull the threads to gather running stitches to fit the doll's waist. Knot thread ends to keep gathers in place. Wrap 12" (30.5cm) of spool wire around the waist to keep it in place on the doll.

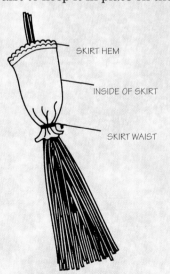

SKIRT HEM

INSIDE OF SKIRT

SKIRT WAIST

(21) Bring skirt down over spool wire wrapping, turning the skirt right side out.

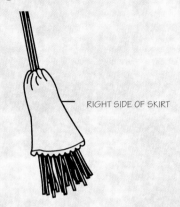

RIGHT SIDE OF SKIRT

ADD HEADS & TRIMS

(22) Using hot glue gun, attach the back of the man's head to the left broom section, with his chin just above the arms. Use the same method to attach the back of the woman's head to the right broom section.

(23) To make the man's rake, cut a 6" (15cm) piece of heavy straw left over from dividing the broom. Use a small piece of spool wire to attach 6 toothpicks to the end of the stick. Secure with a drop of hot glue. Slip the rake into his left-hand loop. Next, use needle and thread to make a 4" (10cm) string of mini red peppers and broken pieces of bay leaf. Tie one end of thread to the farmer's right-hand loop.

(24) Hot glue a few mini red peppers and herb sprigs in the mini basket. Bend a small piece of spool wire around the handle of the basket. Push the spool wire through the woman's hand loop. Twist wire to hold in place.

MAKE BOWS

(25) Use cow-print ribbon to make the bottom bow. Beginning 18" (45.5cm) from one ribbon end, pinch the ribbon between thumb and index finger. Bring ribbon out and back to the center to form a loop. Gather ribbon firmly into your fingers. Make a second loop on the other side of the center. Gather and twist into place.

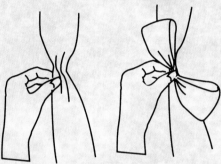

(26) Continue making loops on each side of the center knot until you have 6 loops. Wrap 8" (20.5cm) of spool wire around the center to keep the loops in place. Twist the wire ends to secure. Arrange the loops to shape. Set bow aside.

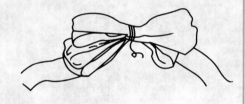

BOW-MAKING TIPS

• If the ribbon you are using is single-sided, twist the ribbon after making each loop. This will show off the right side of the ribbon.

• A rule of thumb for bows: when using wider ribbon, make larger loops.

• To store special bows, place bow in plastic bag, fill with air, and seal bag. Hang to store safely.

27 The top bow is like the bottom bow, except it has a center knot. To make the top bow, use the red gingham ribbon and begin 15" (38cm) from one ribbon end. Begin making the bow, as described above, until you have 4 total loops. Then add a center knot by forming a small circle of ribbon over your thumb. Gather and twist the ribbon in place.

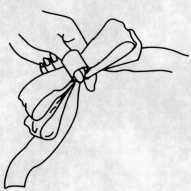

28 Continue making loops on each side of the center knot until you have 8 loops. Wrap a small piece of spool wire through the small center loop and around the bow center to keep the loops in place. Twist the wire ends closed in back.

29 To V-cut streamer ends, fold and cut as shown.

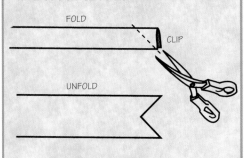

30 Center the top bow on the bottom bow. Wrap 12" (30.5cm) of spool wire around the center. Twist the wire closed in back. Using the photo on page 68 as a guide, wrap the ends of the wire around the broom top to attach the bow. Arrange loops to shape. Bring the streamers down the front of the broom.

31 Wrap a 12" (30.5cm) piece of spool wire around the top of the broom handle under the bow. Twist the two wire ends together to form a loop for hanging broom.

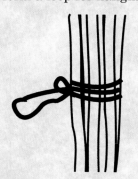

32 Apply a coat of spray-on water and stain repellent, following manufacturer's directions.

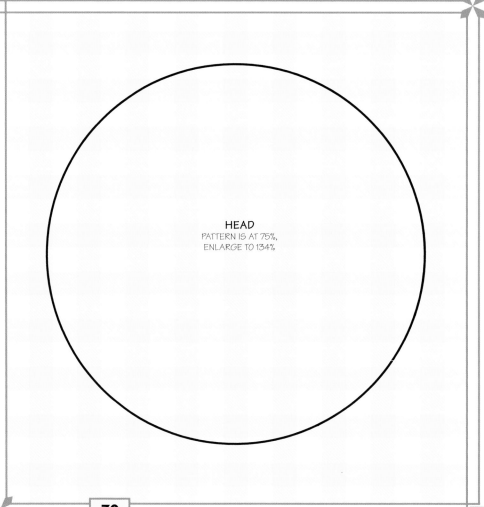

HEAD
PATTERN IS AT 75%,
ENLARGE TO 134%

Blue Denim Dairy Cows

This pair of blue denim cows is headed straight for the family room where they'll accent the casual decor perfectly. The TV Caddy has pockets just the right size to corral the remote control and television program guide. Use matching denim or recycle a pair of old jeans to create acompanion Couch Cow Pillow.

Couch Cow Pillow

YOU WILL NEED

- ⅝ yd (57cm) of denim fabric
- ¼ yd (23cm) of bandanna print fabric
- Bandanna
- Polyester fiberfill
- Two 20mm animal eyes
- Gold stud

CRAFTER'S TIP

A pair of old jeans can be substituted for denim fabric when making any of these projects. Cut the jeans open along the inseams and front crotch seam. Cut the patterns from the legs. Cut out the rear pockets, and substitute them for the pocket patterns if desired.

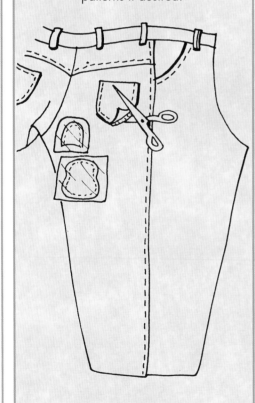

CUT THE FABRIC

① Cut the following pieces from denim: two 11½" × 14½" (29 × 37cm) bodies; three 2" × 15" (5 × 38cm) tail strips; and one 2¼" × 6" (5.7 × 15cm) hair. Cut the following patterns from page 75 from denim: 2 heads, 2 large ears, 1 pocket, and 1 lap pocket. Cut the following patterns on page 74 from bandanna fabric: 4 horns and 2 ears.

MAKE THE HEAD

② Sew each denim ear to a bandanna print ear with right sides together. Leave the bottom open.

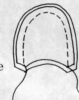

③ Clip the curved seam allowances. Turn each ear right side out, and press. Fold the sides of each ear to the center, overlapping the edges slightly. Pin the ears to one head section between the circle pattern markings.

④ Sew the head sections with right sides together, leaving an opening along the top. Clip the seam allowances.

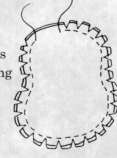

⑤ Turn the head right side out. Stuff firmly with fiberfill. Sew the opening closed by hand. Sew each pair of horn sections with right sides together, leaving the bottom open. Clip the curved seam allowances. Turn right side out. Stuff each horn firmly with fiberfill.

⑥ Turn under the raw edges ¼" (6mm) at the bottom of each horn. Sew the horns to the head between the ears.

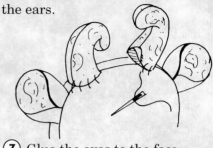

⑦ Glue the eyes to the face.

⑧ Cut a 2" × 6" (5 × 15cm) strip of denim. Cut fine fringe along one long edge for the hair section. Roll up the opposite edge. Glue to the head between horns.

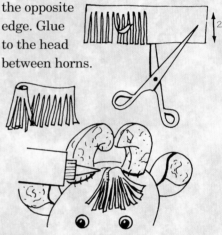

MAKE THE POCKET

⑨ Turn under ⅜" (1cm) on the top and ¼" (6mm) on the straight side edge of the lap pocket. Sew close to each fold and again ¼" (6mm) away. Apply a stud to the lap pocket corner.

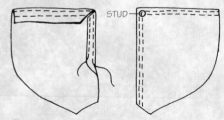

⑩ Pin lap pocket to right side of pocket. Baste the raw edges together. Sew the finished side edge of the lap pocket by hand to the pocket. Turn under ⅜" (1cm) on the top edge and ¼" (6mm) on the remaining edges of the pocket. Sew close to each fold and again ¼" (6mm) away. Trim the corners of the body sections to round them off. Pin the pocket to the right side of one body section. Hand sew in place.

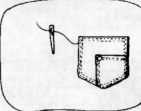

MAKE THE TAIL AND BODY

⑪ Tie the tail strips together at one end with a piece of thread. Cut a fine fringe in the other end of each strip. Braid the strips up to the fringe. Sew across the tip of the tail.

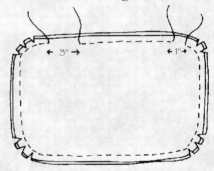

⑫ Sew the body sections with right sides together, leaving a 1" (2.5cm) opening at one top corner for the tail and a 3" (7.5cm) opening for turning near the other top corner. Clip the curved seam allowances. Turn right side out.

← 3" →   ← 1" →

⑬ Insert the tail through the 1" (2.5cm) opening. Hand sew opening closed, catching the tail in the stitches. Stuff the body firmly with fiberfill. Stitch the opening closed. Sew the head to body front. Cut the bandanna diagonally from corner to corner. Tie half of the bandanna around the neck of the cow. Insert the other half into the lap pocket.

TV Caddy

YOU WILL NEED

- ⅜ yd (34.5m) each of denim and bandanna print fabric
- ¼ yd (23cm) of fusible fleece
- 5" (13cm) square of paper-backed fusible web
- 5" (13cm) square of black fabric
- Bandanna
- Two 20mm animal eyes

CUT THE FABRIC

① Cut from bandanna print: one 7½" × 25" (19 × 63.5cm) caddy lining; two 6" × 7½" (15 × 19cm) pocket linings; one 17" × 17" × 32" (43 × 43 × 81cm) triangle for a bandanna; 2 ear patterns, and 4 horn patterns. Reserve the scraps. Cut from denim: one 7½" × 25" (19 × 63.5cm) caddy; two 6" × 7½" (15 × 19cm) pockets; 2 head patterns; and 2 ear patterns. Cut the following from fleece: 2 head patterns and 4 horn patterns.

MAKE APPLIQUÉS

2 Trace the tongue pattern once and the nostril pattern twice onto the paper back of fusible web. Patterns are on the opposite page. Cut out patterns, leaving a small margin of paper all around. Following manufacturer's directions, fuse the tongue shape rough side down onto wrong side of bandanna print fabric. Fuse the nose shapes rough side down onto wrong side of black fabric. Cut out shapes along the traced lines. Do not remove the paper backings.

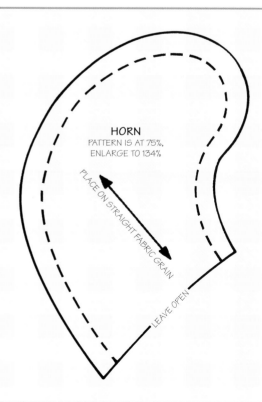

MAKE THE CADDY

3 Sew one long side of each denim pocket to a bandanna print pocket lining with right sides together. Press the seam allowances toward the lining.

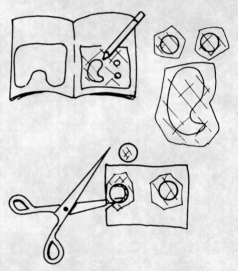

4 Baste a pocket to each end of the denim caddy section. Pin the lining on top with right sides together. Sew a ¼" (6mm) seam around the edges, leaving an opening along one long edge.

5 Turn the caddy right side out. Hand stitch the opening closed. Topstitch through one pocket center.

6 Fold the bandanna in half diagonally. Wrap it around the topstitched pocket, and tie in a knot on one side. Apply a little glue along the front and back of the bandanna.

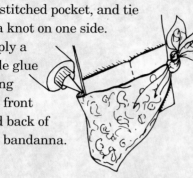

ADD HEAD AND HANDS

7 Peel off paper backings and fuse the tongue and nostrils to right side of one head section. Fuse fleece to the wrong side of each head and horn section.

8 To make the head, see the Couch Cow Pillow on page 72. Place the ears between the circle pattern markings. Sew the horns to the head at the square pattern markings.

9 Sew the head onto the topstitched pocket, over the bandanna.

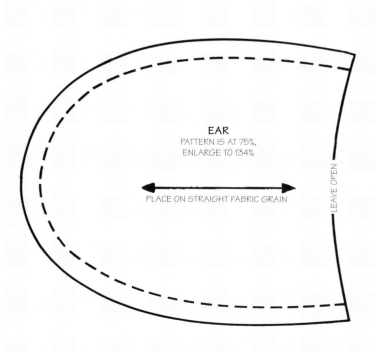

HORN
PATTERN IS AT 75%,
ENLARGE TO 134%

PLACE ON STRAIGHT FABRIC GRAIN

LEAVE OPEN

EAR
PATTERN IS AT 75%,
ENLARGE TO 134%

PLACE ON STRAIGHT FABRIC GRAIN

LEAVE OPEN

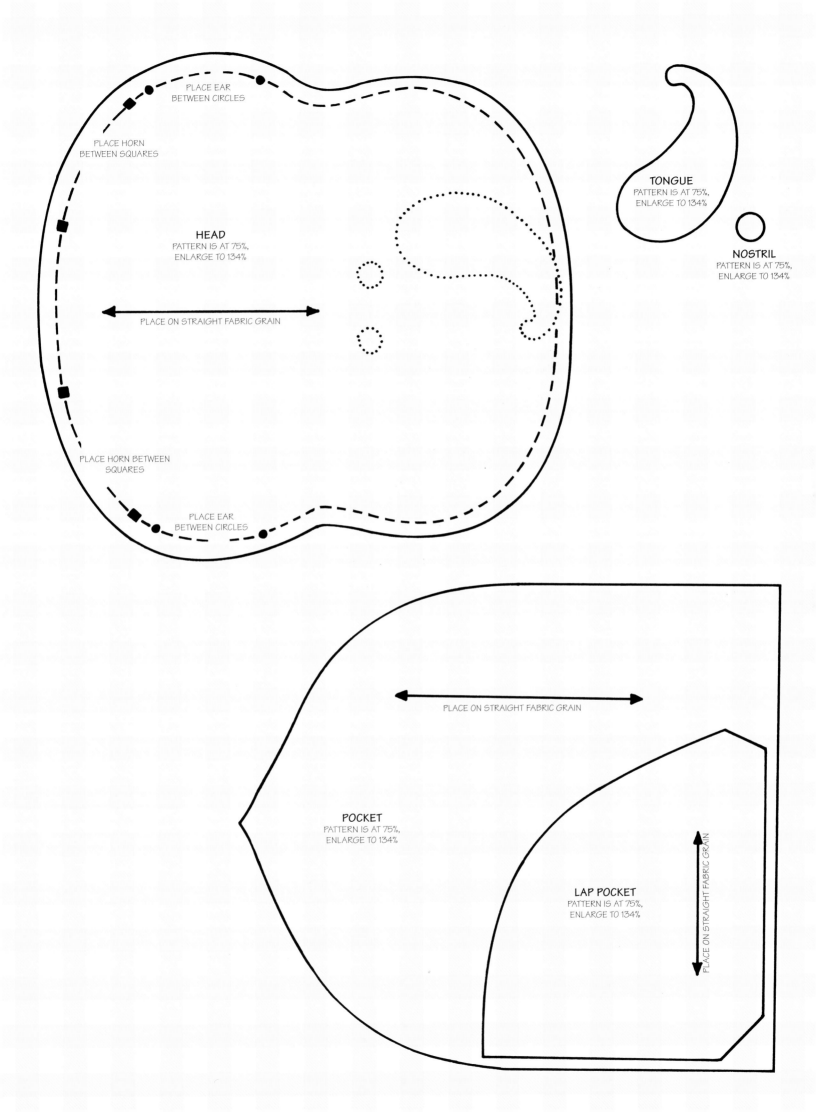

HEAD
PATTERN IS AT 75%,
ENLARGE TO 134%

PLACE EAR
BETWEEN CIRCLES

PLACE HORN
BETWEEN SQUARES

PLACE ON STRAIGHT FABRIC GRAIN

PLACE HORN BETWEEN
SQUARES

PLACE EAR
BETWEEN CIRCLES

TONGUE
PATTERN IS AT 75%,
ENLARGE TO 134%

NOSTRIL
PATTERN IS AT 75%,
ENLARGE TO 134%

PLACE ON STRAIGHT FABRIC GRAIN

POCKET
PATTERN IS AT 75%,
ENLARGE TO 134%

LAP POCKET
PATTERN IS AT 75%,
ENLARGE TO 134%

PLACE ON STRAIGHT FABRIC GRAIN

Potpourri Dolls

Little powder room "rag doll" angels will charm your family and guests. One sweet girl holds hand soaps; the other acts as a fingertip towel. These dolls are wonderful when scented with potpourri!

Soap Basket Doll

YOU WILL NEED

- 8" × 11" (20.5 × 28cm) piece of muslin
- ⅝ yd (57cm) of floral print fabric
- ⅜ yd (34.5cm) of gingham fabric
- 8" (20.5cm) square of polyester batting
- Graphite paper
- 2½" (6.5cm) Styrofoam ball
- Package of curly doll hair
- 1 yd (1m) of gathered lace, 1½" (4cm) wide, for skirt and hat
- 2½ yds (2.5m) of picot-edge ribbon, ¼" (6mm) wide
- Two ⅝" (1.5cm) gathered ribbon roses, for hat and back bow

- Bunch of small silk flowers
- Eleven ½" (1.5cm) gathered ribbon roses for wrists, skirt, and neck
- 28" (71cm) of gathered lace, 2½" (6.5cm) wide, for skirt
- 1¼ yds (1.1m) of picot-edge ribbon, ⅜" (1cm) wide
- 1 cup of potpourri
- 24" (61cm) of gathered lace, ⅝" (1.5cm) wide, for wrists and basket
- 32-gauge spool wire
- Empty, clean margarine container

POTPOURRI TIPS

- Fill the arms or body of your pretty angels with potpourri or potpourri pellets available at your favorite craft store.

- Match the colors of your angel to a special floral potpourri scent. Try a rose scent with pink fabrics and trims, a lavender scent with purples, cinnamon spice with reds, and citrus with yellows and oranges.

- Refresh your potpourri angel with a few drops of potpourri oil.

CUT THE FABRIC

① For the head, cut one 8" (20.5cm) square of muslin. Cut from muslin 4 small hand patterns. Cut from floral print fabric: two medium sleeve patterns; two 9" × 11" (23 × 28cm) pieces for the body; one 8" × 28½" (20.5 × 72cm) piece for the skirt; and one 8" (20.5cm) square for the hat. Cut from gingham three 11" (28cm) squares for the basket lining and cover. Fold the 8" (20.5cm) square of hat fabric in half and then in quarters, and cut 1 flower girl hat pattern. Fold each gingham square in half and then in quarters, and cut 3 basket lining and cover patterns.

MAKE THE HEAD

② Fold muslin and batting squares in half, right sides together, then fold again into quarters. Cut a curved line as shown to make a circle. Unfold.

(3) Fold the muslin circle in half. Place face pattern on the fabric circle as shown.

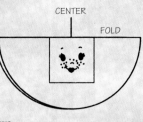

CENTER

FOLD

(4) Slip a piece of graphite paper, graphite side down, between pattern and fabric. Secure graphite paper with masking tape. Using a pencil, trace the face features. Remove the pattern and transfer paper. Draw over the face features with the black marker. Using a cotton swab, brush pink powder blush to cheeks.

(5) Using a needle and thread, make long running stitches ½" (1.5cm) from the edge around the batting circle. Do the same with the muslin circle.

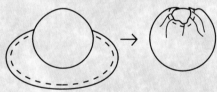

(6) Center the Styrofoam ball on the batting circle. Pull the thread to gather the circle closed around the ball. Pull the gathers as tight as possible without breaking the thread. Knot thread.

(7) Center the covered ball on the muslin circle. Pull the thread to gather the circle closed around the ball. Pull the gathers as tight as possible without breaking the thread. Knot thread to secure. The gathered edges of the circle will be at the neck. Follow manufacturer's directions to apply a coat of spray-on water and stain repellent. Let dry. Hot glue curly doll hair to head.

MAKE THE HAT

(8) Sew running stitches ¼" (6mm) from the edge around the 8" (20.5cm) floral print fabric circle. With face up, center the head on the fabric circle. Pull thread to gather the hat to fit around the head. Knot threads. Hot glue hat to head.

(9) Hot glue 1½" (4cm) wide gathered lace over the hat gathers. Hot glue 8" (20.5cm) of ¼" (6mm) wide picot-edge ribbon over the lace across the hat front. Tie 7" (18cm) of ¼" (6mm) wide picot-edge ribbon into a bow. Glue the bow to the hat. Glue a ⅝" (1.5cm) gathered ribbon rose and 2 small silk flowers to the bow.

MAKE THE BODY

(10) Sew the 2 body sections, right sides together, with a ¼" (6mm) seam allowance. Leave one end open as marked on pattern. Turn body right side out. Stuff with fiberfill. Stitch opening closed.

MAKE THE SKIRT

(11) To make a hem on skirt, turn under one long edge, ⅛" (3mm) and press. Turn under ⅛" (3mm) and press again. Sew along edge.

(12) Stitch or hot glue 2½" (6.5cm) wide gathered lace 2¼" (5.5cm) up from the bottom hem. Glue or sew 1½" (4cm) wide remaining gathered lace over the top edge of the wide lace.

(13) With right sides together, fold the skirt crosswise. Sew the back seam with a ¼" (6mm) seam allowance. Turn skirt right side out. Using a needle and thread, make long running stitches ¼" (6mm) from the raw edge. Pull the thread to gather the fabric slightly.

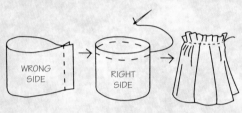

WRONG SIDE

RIGHT SIDE

(14) Slip the skirt waist onto the body and gather waist about 2" (5cm) from body bottom. After gathering, knot thread ends. Hot glue or stitch the gathered skirt waist to the body.

(15) Starting at the back, wrap 10" (25.5cm) of ⅜" (1cm) wide picot-edge ribbon around the waist gathers. Tie 20" (51cm) of ⅜" (1cm) wide picot-edge ribbon in a bow. Glue the bow to the back of waist. Hot glue a ⅝" (1.5cm) gathered ribbon rose on the bow.

BACK VIEW

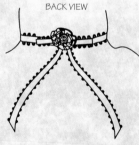

MAKE THE HANDS AND ARMS

16 To make the hands, sew 2 pairs of muslin hand sections along side seams, leaving opening as marked on pattern. Turn and stuff hands firmly with fiberfill. Stitch opening closed. Set hands aside.

17 With right sides together, fold sleeve pieces in half lengthwise. Sew side seams. Turn the sleeves right side out. Use a needle and thread to make a running stitch along short ends of sleeve sections. Pull the thread along sleeve top to gather tightly. Knot thread to secure. Fill both sleeves with potpourri.

18 Pull the thread to gather slightly at the wrist. Fit the end of the stuffed hand inside gathered wrist. Gather tightly and knot. Make small running stitches around the wrists to hold hands in place. Hot glue or stitch ⅝" (1.5cm) wide gathered lace over the wrist gathers.

19 Hot glue the sleeves at either side of the neck with the seam facing down. Wrap 10" (25.5cm) of wire around neck and wrist.

ATTACH THE HEAD AND BASKET

20 Hot glue the head to the body, centered between the shoulders.

21 To make basket lining, make long running stitches ½" (1.5cm) from the edge of one 11" (28cm) gingham fabric circle. Place the lining right side up over the opening of the margarine container. Push the lining down into the container. Pull the thread to gather the lining to fit around the outside of the container. Knot threads.

22 To make basket cover, cut a 1½" (4cm) slit in the center of one of the 2 remaining 11" (28cm) gingham fabric circles.

23 With right sides together, sew a ¼" (6mm) seam to join the two 11" (28cm) fabric circles. Turn the cover right side out through the slit. Hand stitch the slit closed.

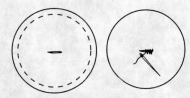

24 Make long running stitches 1¾" (4.5cm) from the edge of the cover. Center the container on top of the cover. Pull the threads to gather the cover to fit the container. Knot threads.

25 Hot glue ⅝" (1.5cm) wide gathered lace over the gathering stitches around the basket cover. Glue ¼" (6mm) wide picot-edge ribbon over the lace. Tie 10" (25.5cm) of ⅜" (1cm) wide picot-edge ribbon into a bow. Glue bow to basket front. Glue a small bunch flowers to the bow. Hot glue the basket under the doll's chin. Hot glue the hands to the sides of the basket.

FINISHING TOUCHES

26 Cut eight 7" (18cm) pieces of ¼" (6mm) wide picot-edge ribbon. Fold each piece in half, overlapping the ribbon to make a 1" (2.5cm) loop. Hot glue the ribbon loops every 4" (10cm) around the lace top on the skirt.

27 Cut two 7" (18cm) pieces of ¼" (6mm) wide picot-edge ribbon and make a bow with each. Glue one bow at each wrist. To make a 4-loop bow, use the remaining ¼" (6mm) wide picot-edge ribbon. Loop one ribbon end, leaving several inches at the bottom for a streamer. Make the second loop in the opposite direction. Make 2 more loops in alternating directions. Wrap a piece of doubled thread around bow center to gather loops. Trim ends if needed.

28 Glue bow neck front. Glue a ½" (1.5cm) ribbon rose to each bow on the skirt, the wrists, and the neck. Follow manufacturer's directions to apply a coat of spray-on water and stain repellent.

Guest Towel Doll

YOU WILL NEED

- 9" × 12" (23 × 30.5cm) piece of muslin
- 7" × 18" (18 × 45.5cm) piece of gingham fabric, for sleeves
- 9" (23cm) square of polyester batting
- Powdered eye shadow
- 3" (7.5cm) Styrofoam ball
- Package of curly doll hair
- 1 yd (91.5cm) of gathered lace, 2½" (6.5cm) wide, for skirt
- 16" (40.5cm) wide hand towel
- ¾ yd (68.5cm) of embroidered ribbon, 1" (2.5cm) wide
- 3" (7.5cm) embroidery hoop
- 2 handfuls of potpourri
- 20" (51cm) of gathered lace, 1½" (4cm) wide, for neck and wrists
- 32-gauge spool wire
- 6" (15cm) doily, for hat
- Corsage pin
- 1 yd (91.5cm) of velvet ribbon, ⅜" (1cm) wide
- Four ½" (1.5cm) ribbon roses
- One ¾" (2cm) ribbon rose
- 12" (30.5cm) of picot-edge ribbon, ⅜" (10mm) wide
- 10" (25.5cm) of satin ribbon, ⅛" (3mm) wide
- 1" (2.5cm) gold heart charm

CUT THE FABRIC

(1) For the head, cut a 9" (23cm) square of muslin. Cut 2 big sleeve patterns from gingham. Cut 4 big hand patterns from muslin.

MAKE THE HEAD AND SKIRT

(2) See Soap Basket Doll to make the head. Set the head aside.

(3) Glue or sew the 2½" (6.5cm) wide gathered lace 2" (5cm) from a short edge of the towel. Wrap ½" (1.5cm) of lace ends around to towel back and sew in place. Sew the other piece of lace 2" (5cm) above the first piece. Sew or glue embroidered ribbon over the top row.

(4) To make the skirt, fold towel in half crosswise. Hand gather the folded edge of the towel with needle and thread. Secure gathers.

(5) Hot glue the gathered edge of towel to bottom half of the inner circle of the embroidery hoop.

MAKE THE HANDS AND ARMS AND ATTACH HEAD

(6) See Soap Basket Doll to make the hands and arms. Hot glue top ends of arms to the towel over the gathers. Glue 5" (13cm) of 1½" (4cm) wide gathered lace around each wrist. With needle and thread, make small stitches to join the hands in front.

(7) Join the ends of a 10" (25.5cm) piece of 1½" (4cm) wide gathered lace to make a loop. Hot glue the lace circle onto the towel between the shoulders. Hot glue head to the body centered on the lace circle.

MAKE THE HAT

(8) To make the hat, fold the 6" (15cm) doily in half. Fold a small tuck in the doily center. Hot glue or stitch to secure. Tie the picot-edge ribbon in a bow. Glue the bow at the center of a 6" (15cm) piece of embroidered ribbon. Glue the ribbon over the tuck on the doily hat. Push a large straight pin through the doily under the bow. Push the pin into the angel's head to attach the doily hat.

FINISHING TOUCHES

(9) Cut four 5" (13cm) pieces of velvet ribbon. Fold 2 pieces in half and hot glue on embroidered ribbon about 5" (13cm) from outer edges of towel. Glue a ½" (1.5cm) ribbon rose on the point of each ribbon. Glue the 2 remaining pieces around the wrists. Glue a ½" (1.5cm) ribbon rose to front of each wrist.

(10) Using the remaining velvet ribbon, see Soap Basket Doll to make a 4-loop bow. Glue bow at neck front under the doll's chin. Glue a ¾" (2cm) ribbon rose on the bow. Thread the ⅛" (3mm) wide satin ribbon through the hole on the heart charm. Tie a bow in the ribbon to make a loop. Glue bow to doll's hands.

(11) Follow manufacturer's directions to apply a coat of spray-on water and stain repellent.

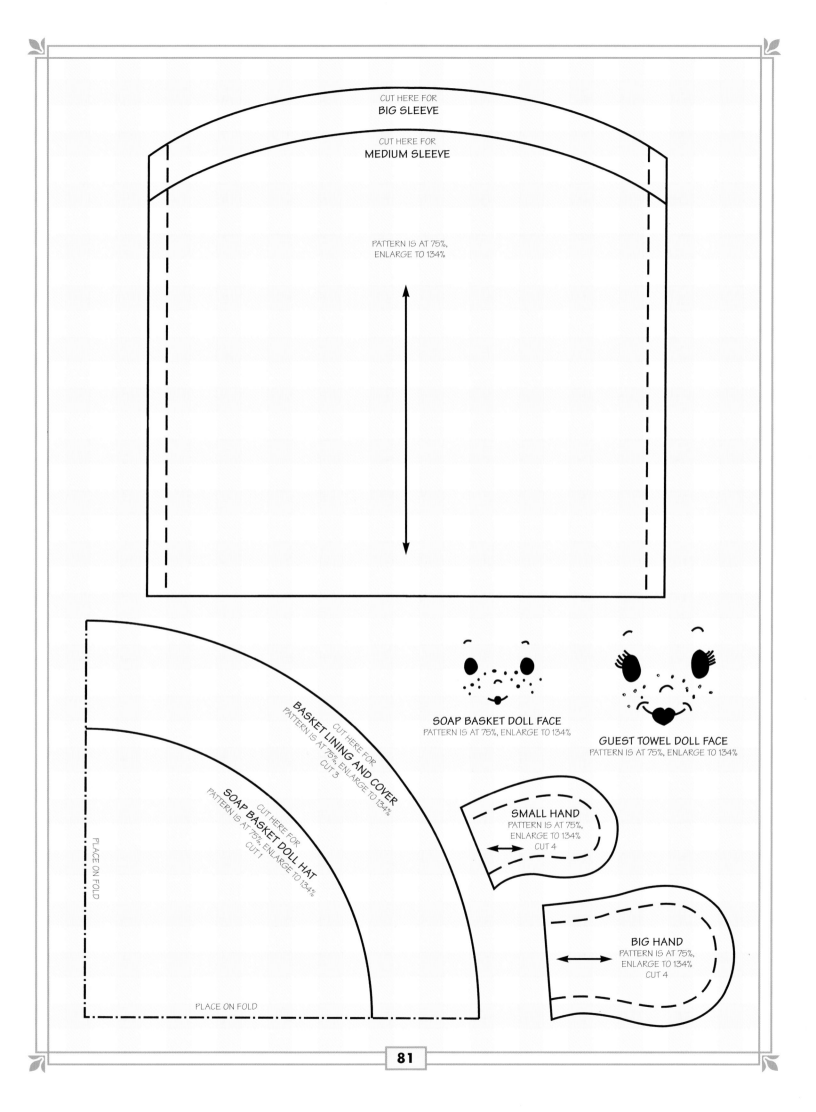

CUT HERE FOR
BIG SLEEVE

CUT HERE FOR
MEDIUM SLEEVE

PATTERN IS AT 75%,
ENLARGE TO 134%

SOAP BASKET DOLL FACE
PATTERN IS AT 75%, ENLARGE TO 134%

GUEST TOWEL DOLL FACE
PATTERN IS AT 75%, ENLARGE TO 134%

CUT HERE FOR
BASKET LINING AND COVER
PATTERN IS AT 75%, ENLARGE TO 134%
CUT 3

CUT HERE FOR
SOAP BASKET DOLL HAT
PATTERN IS AT 75%, ENLARGE TO 134%
CUT 1

PLACE ON FOLD

PLACE ON FOLD

SMALL HAND
PATTERN IS AT 75%,
ENLARGE TO 134%
CUT 4

BIG HAND
PATTERN IS AT 75%,
ENLARGE TO 134%
CUT 4

Gingham Cat Nap Pillow

This soft, sweet cat pillow is content to curl up and nap day and night on any bed, sofa, or easy chair. It's made from gingham fabric, then decorated with eyelet lace and rickrack, as is fitting for a fancy country cat. Create cat nap pillows to accent any room in your home, or to give to your favorite feline fancier.

YOU WILL NEED

- ½ yd (40.5cm) of gingham fabric
- 7" × 12" (18 × 30.5cm) piece of white fabric
- 8" (20.5cm) square of white tulle
- Jumbo rickrack: 1 yd (91.5cm) of one color and ¾ yd (68.5cm) of a contrast color
- Polyester fiberfill
- 2½ yds (2.5m) of gathered lace, 1¾" (4.5cm) wide
- ⅛ yds (11.5cm) of print ribbon, ½" (1.5cm) wide
- Medium rickrack: 4 yds (3.5m) of one color, 2½ yds (2.5m) of a contrast color, and 2 yds (1.8m) of a print
- Colored pencils: light pink and light blue
- ¾ yd (68.5cm) of baby rickrack
- 1" (2.5cm) of purchased appliqué
- Buttons: ten ⅝" (1.5cm) and eight ⁷⁄₁₆" (1.1cm)

CUT FABRIC

① Cut 2 body and 2 tail patterns from gingham. Cut 2 face patterns from white fabric.

MAKE THE FACE

② Place a square of tulle over the actual-size face pattern. Trace the pattern onto the tulle with black marker.

③ Lay the tulle, tracing side up, on the right side of the face section. Hold the tulle in place with one hand as you trace the features onto the face with black marker.

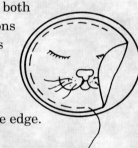

④ Layer both face sections right sides up. Sew them together around the edge.

SEW THE CAT

⑤ Begin at the neck curve to mark one body section with 5 curved lines for trim placement. Space the lines 1" (2.5cm) apart. This is the body front.

⑥ Glue jumbo rickrack along the trim placement lines, alternating the 2 contrasting colors.

7 Pin the face right side up on the right side of one body section. Sew around the edge of the face. This is the body front.

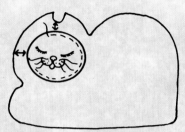

8 Sew the front and back in a ¼" (6mm) seam with right sides together, leaving an opening at the bottom. Clip the seam allowances along curves, being careful not to cut the stitching. Trim diagonally across corners.

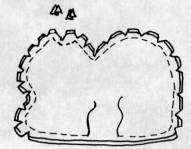

9 Turn right side out. Stuff the cat with fiberfill. Use a stuffing tool to push fiberfill into the ears. Turn under the raw edges ¼" (6mm) at the opening, and slip stitch the opening closed.

10 Start at the bottom to glue lace around outer face edge,

overlapping the ends ½" (1.5cm). In the same way, glue another row of lace overlapping the first row slightly.

11 Start at the bottom to glue print rickrack over the edges of the lace, overlapping the ends ½" (1.5cm). In the same way, glue a row of medium rickrack over the print rickrack.

SEW THE TAIL

12 Sew the tail sections in a ¼" (6mm) seam with right sides together, leaving the base of the tail open. Clip the seam allowances along curves, being careful not to cut the stitching.

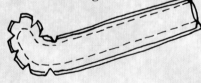

13 Turn right side out. Stuff with fiberfill, using a stuffing tool to push fiberfill into the tip of the tail. Turn the raw edges under ¼" (6mm) at the opening, and slip stitch the opening closed.

14 Start at the base to wrap and glue lace around the tail about 6 times, ending at the tip. Glue print rickrack over the edge of the lace, and medium rickrack over the print rickrack.

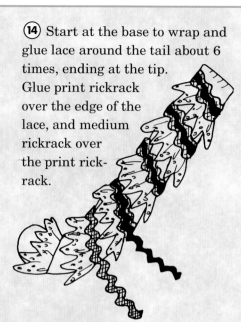

FINISHING TOUCHES

15 Sew the tail to the front of the cat at the lower side edge, with the curved tip of the tail up. Glue the tail along the front of the cat, keeping the lower edges even.

16 Use black marker to draw over the face markings to darken them. Shade the eyelids with light blue pencil. Use light pink pencil to color the nose and mouth and to shade the cheeks.

17 To make a bow, cut three 11" (28cm) pieces of print ribbon and three 14" (35.5cm) pieces of each color of medium rickrack for loops.

Cut one 13" (33cm) piece of print ribbon, three 14" (35.5cm) pieces of each color of medium rickrack, one 10" (25.5cm) piece of print rickrack, and two 13" (33cm) pieces of baby rickrack for streamers.

18 Cut 10" (25.5cm) of spool wire. Fold the ends of each piece of ribbon or trim toward the center to make loops. Overlap the ends ½" (1.5cm) and glue.

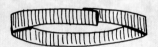

19 Stack the loops in the center of the streamers. Wrap the wire tightly around the center of the loops and streamers to form a bow. Trim all the streamer ends diagonally.

20 Glue the bow below the cat's chin. Glue the appliqué to the center of the bow.

21 Sew thread through the holes of each button in an X. Glue the large buttons to the jumbo rickrack on the cat's body. Glue the small buttons over the rickrack around the face.

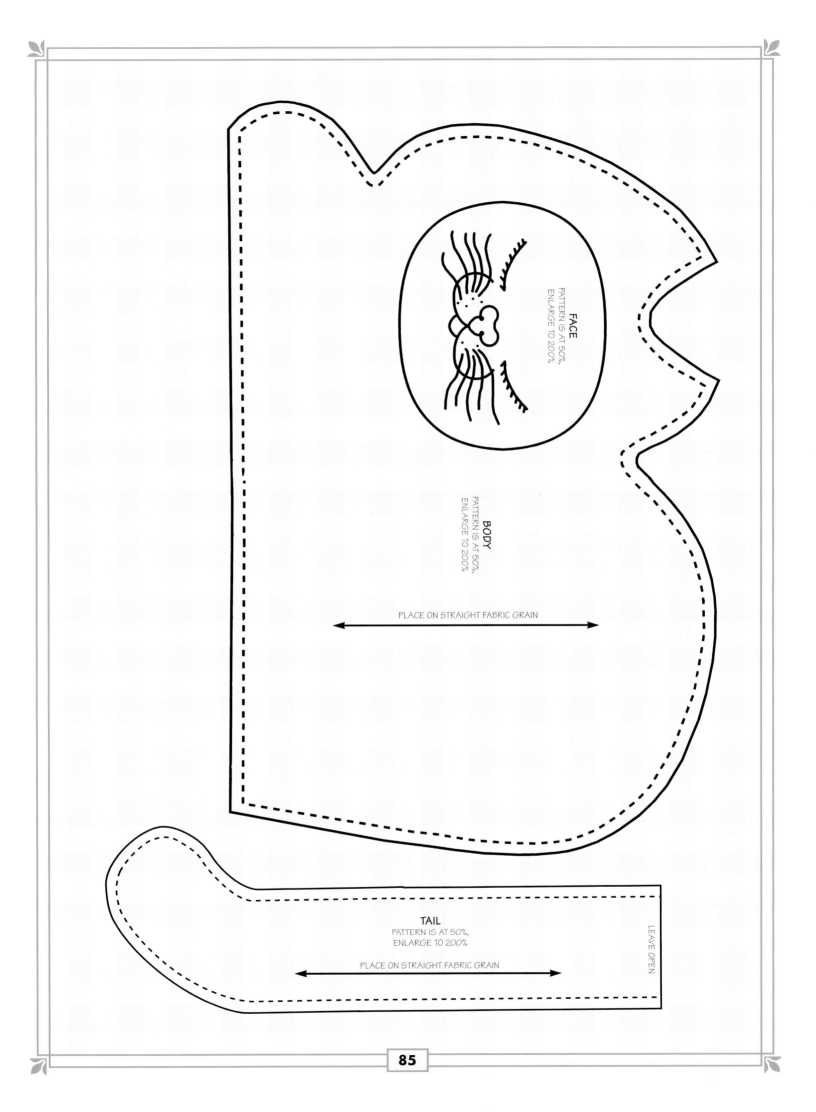

FACE
PATTERN IS AT 50%,
ENLARGE TO 200%

BODY
PATTERN IS AT 50%,
ENLARGE TO 200%

PLACE ON STRAIGHT FABRIC GRAIN

TAIL
PATTERN IS AT 50%,
ENLARGE TO 200%

PLACE ON STRAIGHT FABRIC GRAIN

LEAVE OPEN

Apple Blossoms Recipe and Basket

Begin with fresh, red apples to create these beautiful, handcrafted blossoms for an original basket. Your home will be filled with a wonderful aroma when you slice the apples, then dry them slowly in the oven. The next day, shape the slices into flowers. Combine the apple flowers with dried and silk florals to create a natural arrangement that looks as though it came from your own apple orchard.

Dried Apple Slices Recipe

YOU WILL NEED

- 1 cup (235ml) of lemon juice
- 4 tbs. of salt
- 3 to 7 large, firm apples, such as Rome apples
- Wire baking racks

This recipe yields enough apple slices to complete the basket. Since it takes 4 to 5 hours for the apple slices to dry, you should make them the day before you plan to assemble the project.

DRY THE APPLE SLICES

① Move the oven racks to the highest positions in the oven. Preheat oven to 150° F.

② Mix the lemon juice and salt in a large bowl. Cut the apples into ¼" (6mm) thick slices. Soak them in the lemon juice and salt mixture for 5 minutes, turning them over once. Arrange the slices in a single layer on paper towels. Pat the slices with paper towels to absorb any excess lemon juice and salt mixture.

③ Arrange the slices in a single layer on wire baking racks. Place in the oven for about 4 to 5 hours with the oven door slightly ajar. Remove the slices when they feel dry and leathery. Arrange them in a single layer on paper towels. They should look somewhat shriveled, but still feel pliant. Let the slices dry completely.

These apple slices are purely ornamental. Do not eat them.

Apple Blossoms
Basket

YOU WILL NEED

- Dried apple slices: 7 each of peel and center seed slices
- Spray bottle filled with water
- Clear matte acrylic spray
- 18-gauge spool wire
- Green floral tape
- 2" (5cm) cube of floral foam
- 8" × 15" (20.5 × 38cm) basket with flat back
- Small amount of natural Spanish moss
- Several dried flowers
- 4 silk ivy vines
- Several silk autumn leaves
- Branch of dried eucalyptus
- Paintbrush (optional)
- Walnut stain/sealer (optional)

MAKE FLOWERS

1 Spray a dried apple peel slice and a center seed slice lightly with water for each flower. Place pieces in a 350°F oven for 3 minutes or until pliable. Roll a peel slice, peel side out, into a tight tube for the center of each flower.

2 Cut the seeds out of the center of a center seed slice for the outside of each flower, and roll into a cup. Glue the edges where they overlap.

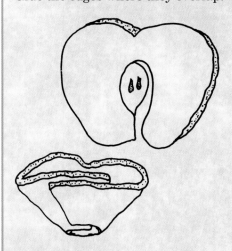

CRAFTER'S TIP

If an aged, antique look is desired, brush a light coat of walnut stain/sealer onto the basket and let dry overnight before adding any decorations.

③ Push each center about halfway into the hole at the bottom of each cup and glue.

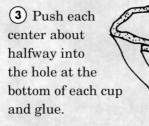

④ Spray each flower with acrylic spray. Place on a wire rack until dry to the touch.

⑤ Cut 7 pieces of wire, varying the lengths from 5"–12" (12.3 to 30.5cm). Push a piece of wire up through the center of the blossom until it sticks out about 2" (5cm). Use pliers to bend the top of the wire into a small hook. Pull the bottom of the wire down to hide the hook in the center of the blossom.

⑥ Starting at the base of the blossom, wrap floral tape around the base and wire to form the stem.

⑦ Spray each blossom with a very light coat of acrylic spray. Let the sprayed flowers dry overnight.

FILL THE BASKET

⑧ Glue the foam block into the basket. Glue Spanish moss around the top and sides of the block to cover it. Glue one ivy vine along one side of the basket handle. Apply glue to one end of the remaining ivy vines, and push the vines into the foam block so that they drape over the basket edges.

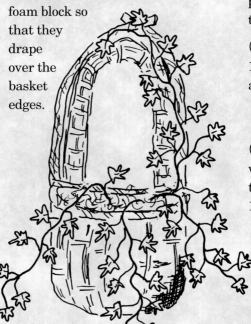

⑨ Apply glue to the end of each flower stem, then push the flowers into the foam block. Place the longer stems near the back and the shorter stems near the front.

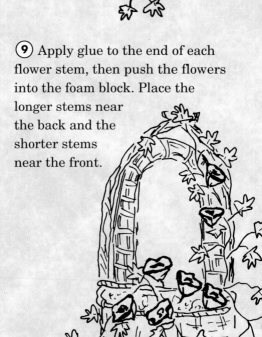

⑩ Glue the leaves and dried flowers into the foam block to fill in the spaces between the flowers. Arrange some of the leaves to drape over the basket edges. Cut the eucalyptus into 3 pieces, each a different size. Apply glue to one end of each piece. Then, push the pieces into the foam block near the back of the basket.

⑪ To make a hanging loop, fold 10" (25.5cm) of spool wire in half and twist.

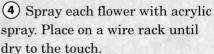

⑫ Fold the twisted wire in half, and twist to form a 1" (2.5cm) loop.

⑬ Twist the wire ends into the top of the handle.

Shade Makeovers

An interesting small lamp can add just the right touch to a room. If you have an ordinary new lamp, or a garage sale find that needs a makeover, you can do it in minutes. It's easy to make a unique new lampshade with peel-and-stick adhesives and paint or fabric. Choose fabric and paint colors that coordinate with your room for a custom decorator accent.

Pretty Pleats

YOU WILL NEED

- 13" × 18" (33 × 45.5cm) piece of fabric
- 13" × 18" (33 × 45.5cm) piece of white paper
- 13" × 18" (33 × 45.5cm) piece of paper-backed fusible web
- Hole punch
- 1 yd (91.5cm) of double fold bias tape, ¼" (6mm) wide
- 3" × 5¼" × 8" (7.5 × 13 × 20.5cm) plain lampshade
- 1½ yds (1.4m) of daisy trim

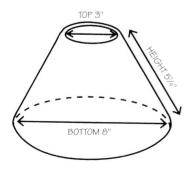

TOP 3"
HEIGHT 5¼"
BOTTOM 8"

FUSE AND MEASURE

① Fold fabric, paper, and fusible web in half lengthwise. Cut each piece along fold line to make two 6½" × 18" (16.5 × 45.5cm) pieces. Fuse white paper to wrong side of fabric following the manufacturer's directions.

② Place fused fabric, paper side up. Measure and mark every 1" (2.5cm) along the long edges of each piece. Use a ruler to draw light pencil lines, connecting the dots.

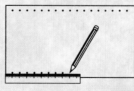

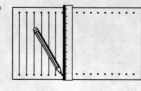

MAKE PLEATS

③ Fold paper over ruler edge along the pencil lines to make accordion pleats on each piece, starting with the paper side facing up.

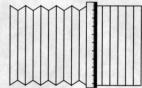

④ To connect the 2 pieces, overlap one pleated edge onto the other.

⑤ Be sure fabric pattern runs in the same direction on both pieces. Glue edges together.

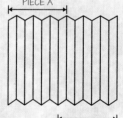

PIECE A
PIECE B

ABOUT LIGHT BULBS

Use a 40- to 60-watt bulb with these lampshades.

CRAFTER'S TIP

For neat gluing and a strong bond, use a glue gun with a small tip and glue sticks made especially for fabric.

PUNCH HOLES

6 Use pencil to lightly mark paper side on each pleat, 1" (2.5cm) from top edge and centered between the folds. Pinch both sides of pleat together. Use the hole punch to punch a hole through both layers.

COVER THE SHADE

7 Overlap and glue pleated ends together to form a ring. The glued pleat will be the back of the shade cover. Top and bottom edges should be even. Beginning in back, on inside of hole, thread bias tape through the holes as shown.

8 Gently pull bias ends to gather top of shade so that the diameter of the top opening is about 3" (7.5cm) wide. Tie bias tape ends into a bow.

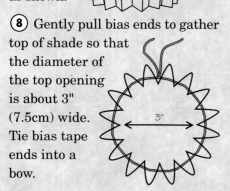

9 Turn pleated cover upside down. Put the plain shade inside the cover. Hot glue the inside pleats to top and bottom rims of lampshade. Let dry.

10 Glue daisy trim around bottom edge of pleated shade cover.

Country Garden

YOU WILL NEED

- 4" × 11" × 7½" (10 × 28 × 19cm) self-adhesive lampshade
- 15" × 25" (38 × 63.5cm) piece of print fabric or paper, for shade
- Hot glue gun and glue sticks
- 24-gauge spool wire
- 1 yd (1m) of matching print fabric, for base
- Several strands of natural raffia

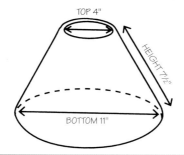

TOP 4"

HEIGHT 7½"

BOTTOM 11"

CUT THE SHADE COVER

1 Peel paper shade cover off the self-adhesive lampshade and use it as a pattern. Place pattern on wrong side of desired fabric or paper. Cut fabric or paper, leaving a 1" (2.5cm) border on the top and bottom edges.

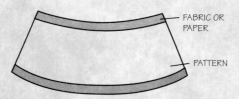

FABRIC OR PAPER

PATTERN

APPLY THE COVER

2 To apply cover, hold the short ends in each hand. Place the cover center on the lampshade center, opposite the back seam. Roll the cover over the shade until the ends meet in back. Smooth fabric or paper with hands.

3 Cut slits in the extended edges to the shade rim, at the top and bottom. Make slits about 1"–2" (2.5–5cm) apart, depending on the size of the shade. Fold over tabs and hot glue to inside of shade.

TOP VIEW

COVER THE LAMP BASE

4 Measure lamp base from one side of neck to the opposite side as shown, then add 10" (25.5cm). Cut a fabric square equal to this measurement.

5 Fold fabric in half, then fold into quarters. Draw a curved line as shown, then cut along line.

6 Open up fabric circle and place lampshade in the center. Cut a 1" (2.5cm) slit to pass the lamp cord through.

7 Pull up fabric over base and gather at top with wire. If needed, cut excess fabric about 1" (2.5cm) above wire. Tie raffia into a bow around base.

TRY THIS!

We used a self-adhesive lampshade to make the Country Garden lamp. If you prefer, you can use double-sided adhesive sheets to attach paper or fabric to a plain lampshade. Adhesive sheets are repositionable and do not require drying time.

TRY THIS!

After making a new lampshade, you may want to "liven up" or replace an old lamp base. You can cover the base with fabric as described in the Country Garden lamp project, or you can apply a coat of acrylic paint to a plain wood base. Be creative and use other paint techniques to add texture to the base. Try sponge painting, faux finishes, or antiquing. Wood lamp bases are available at your favorite craft store.

Plump Pillow Apple Wreath

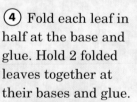

A wreath is a friendly welcome when hung on a door and a bright and cheerful accent on a wall or cabinet. This easy-to-sew wreath is made from plump little fabric pillows in the shape of apples.

YOU WILL NEED

- ½ yd (45.5cm) of red and white print fabric
- ¼ yd (23cm) green print fabric
- Polyester fiberfill
- 9" (23cm) wire macramé ring or embroidery hoop
- ⅜ yd (34.5cm) of satin ribbon, ⅜" (1cm) wide

CUT FABRIC

① Cut 12 apple patterns from red and white fabric. Cut 24 leaf patterns from green fabric. For apple pillows, cut a 2" (5cm) slit for turning in 6 of the pillow sections.

MAKE PILLOWS

② Sew pairs of slit and unslit pillow sections with right sides together with a ¼" (6mm) seam. Clip the seam allowances at curves. Turn each pillow right side out. Use a stuffing tool to turn corners completely. Stuff each pillow firmly with fiberfill. Use a stuffing tool to fill any points or tight spots.

③ Stitch each pair of leaves with right sides together with a ¼" (6mm) seam. Leave the straight edges open. Trim the seam allowances across each corner and clip the curves. Turn each leaf right side out. Use a stuffing tool to turn out the points.

④ Fold each leaf in half at the base and glue. Hold 2 folded leaves together at their bases and glue.

⑤ Glue a pair of leaves behind each apple.

⑥ To attach the apple pillows to the ring or hoop, lay a pillow face down. Place the ring or hoop over the slit. Insert a threaded needle into the pillow just above the ring. Bring the needle out just below the ring. Pull the thread slightly to begin to close the slit. Take a stitch over the ring or hoop. Insert the needle through the pillow, about ¼" (6mm) from the first stitch.

⑦ Continue to stitch across the back of the pillow, closing the slit as you sew the pillow to the ring or hoop. Add another pillow after the first one is securely attached. Do not break the thread between pillows. Add the remaining pillows in the same way to cover the ring or hoop.

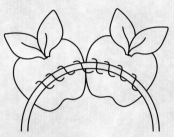

⑧ Glue the side edges of neighboring apples together.

⑨ Fold satin ribbon in half. Slip the folded edge of the ribbon under the wreath, pull the ends through the loop, and pull to tighten.

⑩ Hold the wreath up to decide where to knot the hanging loop. Tie the ends of the ribbon together in a knot at this point. Cut away extra ribbon to leave 1" (2.5cm) tails. Trim the ribbon ends diagonally.

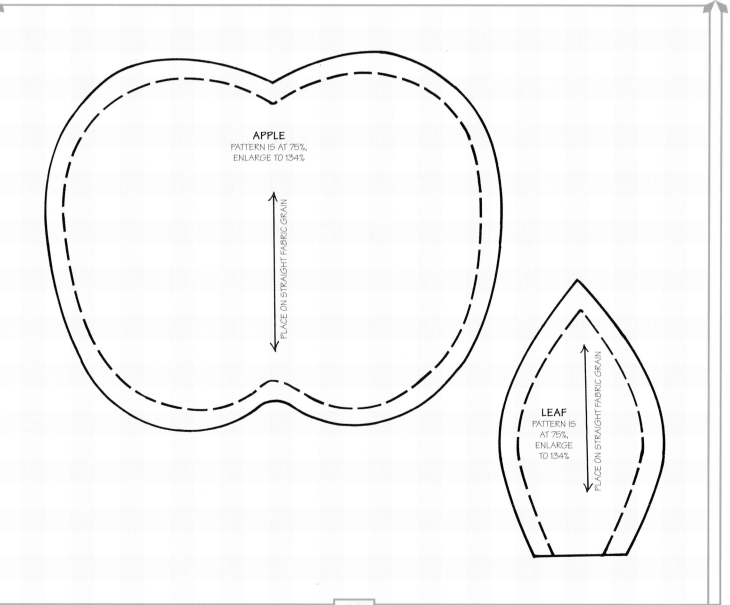

APPLE
PATTERN IS AT 75%,
ENLARGE TO 134%

PLACE ON STRAIGHT FABRIC GRAIN

LEAF
PATTERN IS AT 75%, ENLARGE TO 134%

PLACE ON STRAIGHT FABRIC GRAIN

Chapter Five

Housewarming Treasures

HONEY

SEEDS

Coffee, Tea, and Potpourri

Decorate with country fabrics and inviting fragrances by creating pretty fabric hot pads with the sweet aroma of scented potpourri! These easy appliqué projects are perfect for your coffee-loving friends and make welcome gifts for a neighbor's country kitchen.

Coffee Mug

YOU WILL NEED

- 9" × 22" (23 × 56cm) piece of print fabric (A), for mug
- 3" × 13" (7.5 × 33cm) piece of beige fabric (B), for mug interior and handle
- 9" × 11" (23 × 28cm) piece of paper-backed fusible web
- 9" × 11" (23 × 28cm) piece of unbleached muslin
- Two 9" × 11" (23 × 28cm) pieces of fusible fleece
- 9" × 11" (23 × 28cm) piece of white tulle
- 9" × 11" (23 × 28cm) piece of tear-away stabilizer
- Handful of potpourri

ABOUT APPLIQUÉ FABRICS

- Use light- to medium-weight fabrics in solid colors or small-scale prints.

- For best results, prewash fabric in cold water to preshrink. Tumble dry and press before beginning the project.

- Our potpourri hot pads are made from coordinating fabrics. For creative crafting, use photos as a guide, then feel free to substitute fabrics of your choice for the styles and colors shown.

ABOUT PATTERNS

Note that the appliqué patterns are reverse images of the shapes as they appear in the photographs. When traced onto the paper backing, then fused in place, these shapes will be reversed to match the photographs.

CUT PATTERNS

① Cut a 9" × 11" (23 × 28cm) piece of fabric A and set it aside to use later for the backing. Trace mug, mug interior, and mug handle onto the smooth paper side of the fusible web. Cut out each shape, leaving a small margin of paper around the shape.

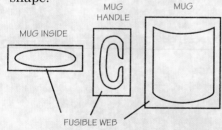

FUSE APPLIQUÉS

② Place appliqué fabrics right side down on the ironing board. Place the fusible web shape, rough side down, on the fabric. Following the manufacturer's directions, fuse the web to the fabric. Cut out the shapes along the solid lines.

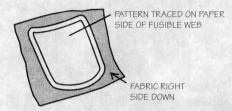

PATTERN TRACED ON PAPER SIDE OF FUSIBLE WEB

FABRIC RIGHT SIDE DOWN

③ Following the fusible web manufacturer's directions, peel off the paper backings and fuse the appliqués to the muslin piece as follows: fuse mug to muslin center. Fuse handle and mug interior. Following the manufacturer's directions, apply fusible fleece to the wrong side of the appliquéd muslin piece and the backing fabric piece.

TRACE STITCHING PATTERN

④ Place white tulle over pattern. Using a disappearing marker, trace onto tulle the pattern outline and interior sew lines.

⑤ Turn each tracing over and position it over the corresponding fused appliqué. Using a disappearing marker, retrace the interior sew lines onto the appliqué shape. Remove the netting before sewing.

SATIN STITCH

⑥ To satin stitch, adjust the sewing machine to make a short, ⅛" (3mm) wide zigzag stitch. Use a standard zigzag presser foot. Pin the appliquéd muslin piece right side up on the tear-away stabilizer. Using the photo opposite as a guide, satin stitch along all interior sew lines and interior shape edges. Machine baste less than ⅛" (3mm) from the outer edge of appliqués. Tear away the stabilizer both inside and outside the stitching.

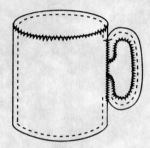

ADD POTPOURRI AND BACKING

⑦ Place the muslin piece right side down on your work surface. Sprinkle a handful of potpourri within the basted shape. With wrong sides together, pin the backing fabric piece over the appliquéd muslin piece so that the potpourri is sandwiched between layers of batting. Carefully flip over to show right side of appliquéd muslin. Using a short, ⅛" (3mm) wide zigzag stitch, satin stitch around the outer edges of the appliqués, covering the machine basting. Using small, sharp scissors, trim fabric around the outside edges of the appliqués close to the satin stitching. To finish any raw edges, make a second row of satin stitching over the first outer edge stitching.

ABOUT SATIN STITCHING

• To satin stitch around interior detail curves, stop stitching with the needle in the top appliqué piece. Raise the presser foot, pivot the appliqué slightly, then lower the presser foot to resume stitching. Stop and pivot the appliqué often to stitch smooth curves.

• To satin stitch around interior detail corners, stop stitching ⅛" (3mm) past a corner on the top appliqué piece. Raise the presser foot with the needle in the appliqué, pivot the fabric, then lower the presser foot to resume stitching.

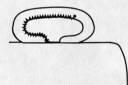

• To satin stitch around outer edge curves, stop stitching with the needle in the muslin or white fabric. Raise the presser foot, pivot the fabric slightly, then lower the presser foot to resume stitching. Stop and pivot the fabric often to stitch smooth curves.

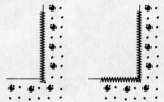

• To satin stitch around outer edge corners, stop stitching at the corner with the needle in the muslin or white fabric. Raise the presser foot to pivot the fabric, then lower the presser foot to resume stitching.

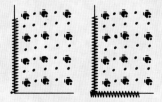

Coffee Pot

Fruit Pie Slice

MAKE A FRUIT PIE SLICE

① See Coffee Mug to cut the following patterns: one entire pie shape from each fabric A and B. Cut out vent holes and pie filling area from fabric A only. See Coffee Mug to fuse appliqués to muslin in the following order: fuse fabric B to the muslin. Fuse fabric A over fabric B. Follow the remaining steps from Coffee Mug to finish the pie slice.

YOU WILL NEED

- 9" × 22" (23 × 56cm) piece of blue print fabric (A), for coffee pot
- 4" × 5" (10 × 13cm) piece of red print fabric (B), for heart
- 2" × 4" (5 × 10cm) piece of beige print fabric (C), for handle
- 9" × 16" (23 × 40.5cm) piece of paper-backed fusible web
- 9" × 11" (23 × 28cm) piece of unbleached muslin
- Two 9" × 11" (23 × 28cm) pieces of fusible fleece
- 9" × 11" (23 × 28cm) piece of tear-away stabilizer
- Handful of potpourri

YOU WILL NEED

- 9" × 22" (23 × 56cm) piece of red check fabric (A), for pie, vent holes and filling
- 9" × 22" (23 × 56cm) piece of red print fabric (B), for pie
- Two 9" × 11" (23 × 28cm) pieces of paper-backed fusible web
- 9" × 22" (23 × 56cm) piece of unbleached muslin
- 9" × 11" (23 × 28cm) piece of tear-away stabilizer
- Handful of fruit- or berry-scented potpourri

MAKE A COFFEE POT

① See the Coffee Mug to cut the following patterns: 1 coffee pot, one heart, and 1 coffee pot handle. Fuse appliqués to muslin in the following order: fuse coffee pot to muslin center. Fuse heart to coffee pot center. Fuse handle centered ½" (1.5cm) above coffee pot. Follow the remaining steps from Coffee Mug to finish.

ABOUT POTPOURRI

Match the colors and design of your hot pad to a special flower or spice potpourri scent. You can find potpourri in many different scents at your local craft store.

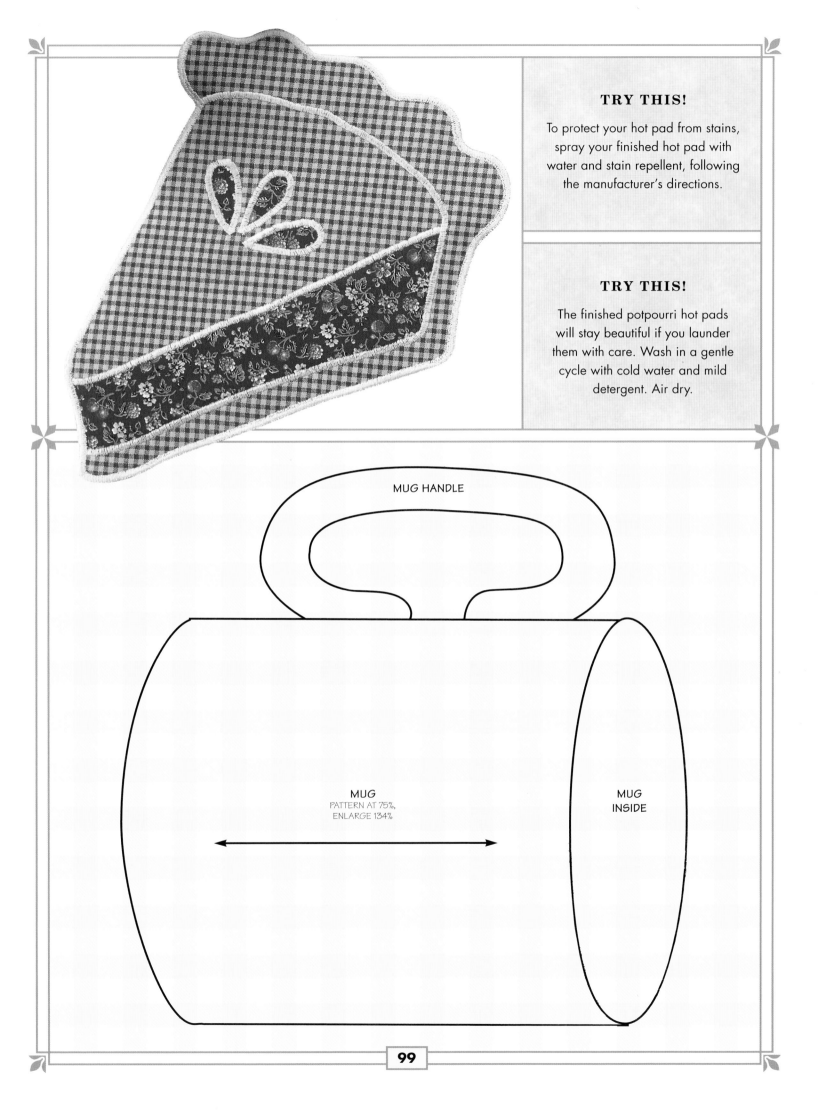

MUG HANDLE

MUG
PATTERN AT 75%,
ENLARGE 134%

MUG
INSIDE

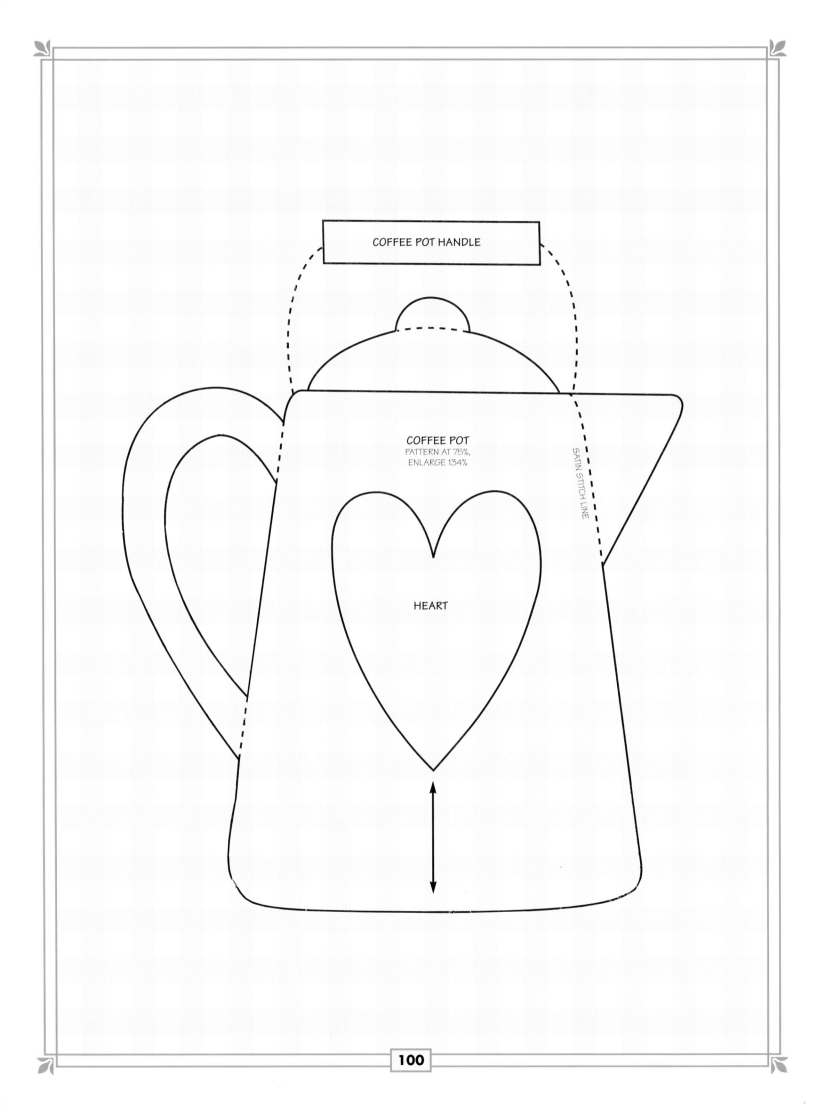

COFFEE POT HANDLE

COFFEE POT
PATTERN AT 75%,
ENLARGE 134%

SATIN STITCH LINE

HEART

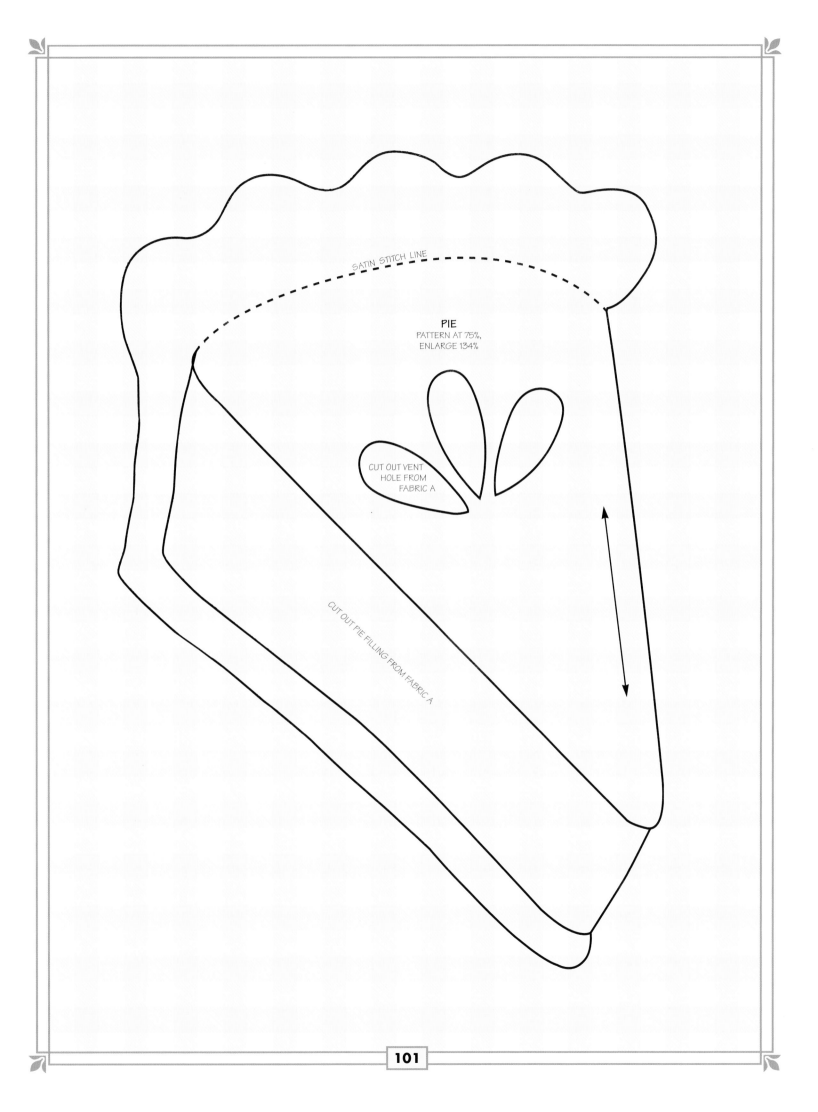

SATIN STITCH LINE

PIE
PATTERN AT 75%,
ENLARGE 134%

CUT OUT VENT
HOLE FROM
FABRIC A

CUT OUT PIE FILLING FROM FABRIC A

Our Family Fabric Wreath

No matter how large or small your family is, you can craft a personalized wreath to symbolize the close ties among its members. Craft the central couple figures from muslin, cardboard, and batting. Around the wreath, arrange large and small wood hearts to name the second and third generations. It's a wonderful way to celebrate your family and a thoughtful remembrance for anniversaries or other special occasions. It's sure to become a family heirloom.

YOU WILL NEED

- 1½" (4cm) wood letters
- 1½" (4cm) wood hearts
- ½ yd (45.5cm) of natural muslin
- 12" × 30" (30.5 × 76cm) piece of cardboard
- 12" × 30" (30.5 × 76cm) piece of batting
- Acrylic paints in white, rose, and gray or colors as desired
- 3 yds (2.7m) of ruffled ecru lace, ¾" (2cm) wide
- Small flat paintbrush
- Dimensional writer paints in white, rose, blue, black, and brown
- Small tapered paintbrush
- 7" (18cm) of picture-hanging wire
- 18" (45.5cm) grapevine wreath

MAKE A FAMILY TREE

① To make a family tree, fill in the chart to plan the arrangement of names on the wreath and to make a shopping list for wood letters and hearts. Begin with the family surname. You will need enough wood letters to spell out the surname at the top of the wreath.

② Next, list the names you'll write on the medium heart held by the female figure in the center. In a traditional family, the grandparents' names are written here. For a not-so-traditional family, this heart might name the oldest or most honored member of the household.

FAMILY WREATH CHART

FAMILY SURNAME: _____

GRANDPARENTS' FIRST NAMES: _____

PARENTS' FIRST NAMES:

HEART #1	HEART #2	HEART #3	HEART #4
_____	_____	_____	_____
_____	_____	_____	_____

CHILDREN'S NAMES:

_____ | _____ | _____ | _____
_____ | _____ | _____ | _____
_____ | _____ | _____ | _____
_____ | _____ | _____ | _____

③ Finally, write down the names that will go on the large and small hearts around the outside of the wreath. In a traditional family, the large hearts name the parents, and the small hearts name their children. For a not-so-traditional family, label the hearts in a personal and creative way to reflect the various relationships.

④ Once the chart has been filled in, you can count the number of wood letters, large hearts, and small hearts you will need.

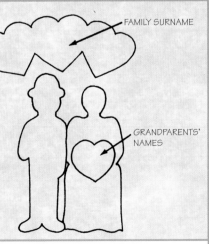

FAMILY SURNAME

GRANDPARENTS' NAMES

PARENTS' NAMES

CHILD'S NAME

PARENTS' NAMES

CHILD'S NAME

CUT THE FABRIC AND CARDBOARD

① Cut the triple heart, the medium heart, the male figure, and the female figure once from muslin. Cut on the broken outline of each pattern to include a ¼" (6mm) seam allowance, and place the patterns on the bias grain of the muslin. Cut the large heart as many times as needed from muslin, cutting on the pattern's broken outline. Also cut a 4" × 5" (10 × 13cm) piece of muslin for the female figure's apron.

① Cut the triple heart, the medium heart, the male figure, and the female figure once each from cardboard and batting. Cut on the solid outline of each pattern, since no seam allowance is needed. Cut the large heart as many times as needed from cardboard and batting, cutting on the pattern's solid outline. Use dressmaker's carbon paper and a tracing wheel to transfer all the pattern markings to the right side of the muslin male and female figures.

GLUE AND PAINT

① Glue batting to each cardboard cutout. Lay each cardboard cutout, batting side down, on the wrong side of the matching muslin piece. Wrap the muslin around the cardboard, clipping the seam allowance around the curves. Glue the muslin to the back of the cardboard. Let the glue dry.

① Apply 2 coats of white paint to the front of all the wood letters, hearts, and figures. Let the paint dry thoroughly after each coat. Mix rose with white to paint the letters pink. Paint the small wood hearts and the medium heart rose. Let the paints dry. Paint alternating blue and rose dots around the edge of the triple heart and the large hearts with a toothpick.

ROSE · BLUE

① Glue the lace around the back of each large heart and the triple heart, overlapping the ends at center top.

① Use a flat brush to paint the various colored areas on the male figure. Mix gray paint with white to paint the man's hat and shirt light gray. Thin a small amount of brown with water to paint the face and hands. Leave the remaining areas white. Let the paint dry. Draw the details on his clothing with a black dimensional paint writer.

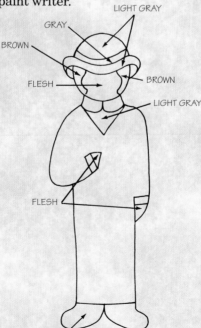

LIGHT GRAY
GRAY
BROWN
FLESH
BROWN
LIGHT GRAY
FLESH
BLACK

① Use dimensional writer paints to draw the clothing outlines and clothing details on the female figure. Also, paint the top of the head blue for her hat, and paint her hair brown. Thin a small amount of brown paint with water to make flesh-toned paint for her face and hands. Thin a small amount of rose with water to make blush for her cheeks.

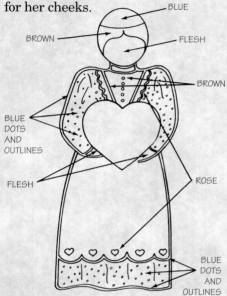

BLUE
BROWN
FLESH
BROWN
BLUE DOTS AND OUTLINES
FLESH
ROSE
BLUE DOTS AND OUTLINES

① Paint white eyes on the male and female figures. Paint a blue or brown pupil in each eye. Paint a black edge along the bottom of each pupil. With a toothpick, paint a white spot on each pupil. Begin at the inside corner of each eye to paint black lashes. Mix rose and white paints to make a pink dot at the inside corner with a toothpick and a thin pink line along the bottom of each eye. Let the paints dry.

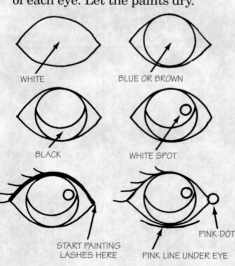

WHITE · BLUE OR BROWN
BLACK · WHITE SPOT
START PAINTING LASHES HERE · PINK DOT · PINK LINE UNDER EYE

⑬ Use a tapered brush to paint the remaining details on the clothes and faces. Refer to photograph on page 103 as a color key. Mix brown and white paints for light highlights on the hair, or mix brown and black for dark highlights. Let paint dry. Use dimensional writer paints for details on the eyes and faces.

⑭ Glue lace around 3 sides of the apron. Pleat the top of the apron, and glue it to the female figure.

⑮ Glue lace along the edge of the hat.

WRITE NAMES AND ASSEMBLE WREATH

⑯ Write the names on the large and medium heart with an evaporating ink fabric marker. Trace the names with a white dimensional paint writer. Let the paint dry. Write the names on each small wood heart lightly with pencil. Trace each name with a white dimensional paint writer. Let the paint dry.

⑰ Fold the wire in half twice. Twist the wire several times to make a hanging loop about ¾" (2cm) long. Twist the ends of the loop around several vines at the center top of the wreath.

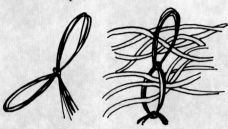

⑱ Glue the wood letters across the triple heart. Then glue the triple heart to the center top of the wreath. Glue the medium heart to the female figure, and glue the male and female figures in the center of the wreath. Glue the small hearts to the large hearts, and glue the large hearts around the sides of the wreath.

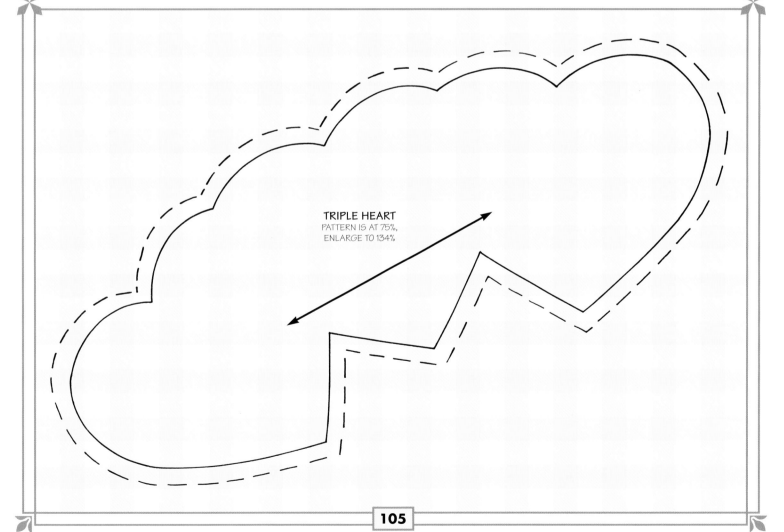

TRIPLE HEART
PATTERN IS AT 75%,
ENLARGE TO 134%

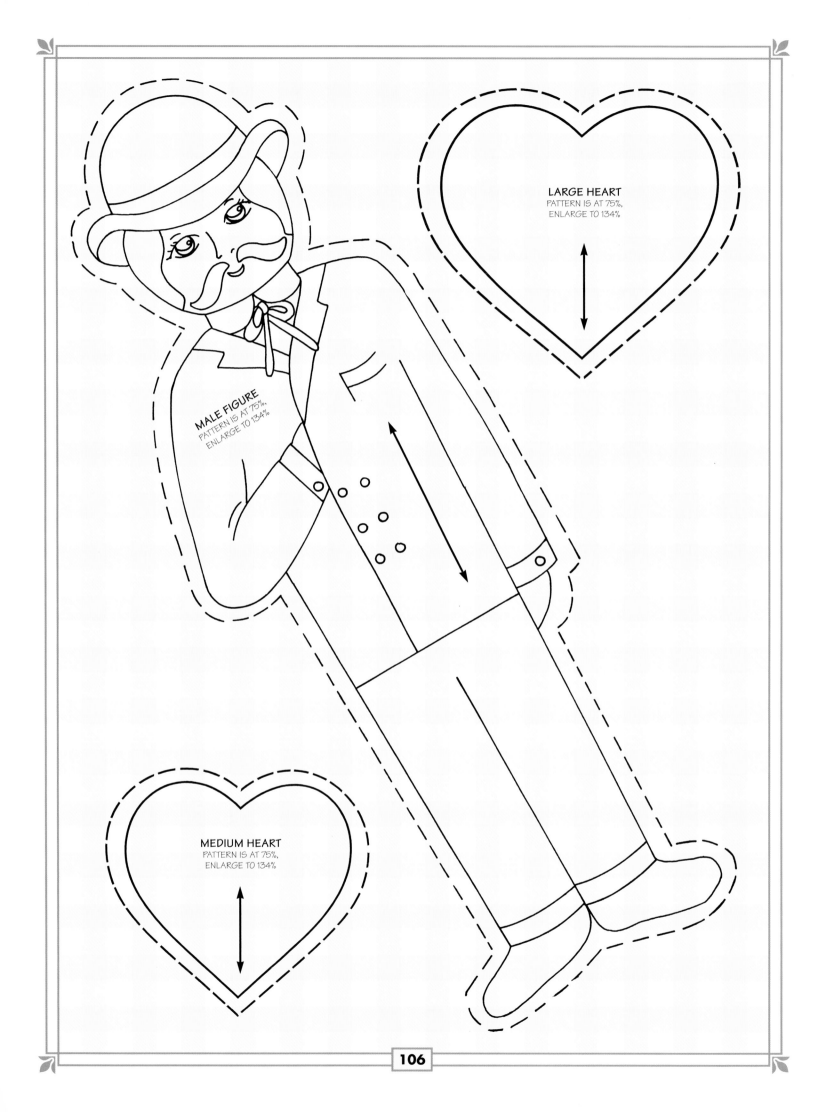

LARGE HEART
PATTERN IS AT 75%,
ENLARGE TO 134%

MALE FIGURE
PATTERN IS AT 75%,
ENLARGE TO 134%

MEDIUM HEART
PATTERN IS AT 75%,
ENLARGE TO 134%

PAINTING LINE FOR HAT
ON FABRIC FIGURE ONLY

FEMALE FIGURE
PATTERN IS AT 75%,
ENLARGE TO 134%

Bee My Honey Gift Sack

Your morning will start with a smile if this sweet sack is on your breakfast table. It's a cute centerpiece and a neat catch-all at the same time. Put flowers in the small basket, then stash sweeteners, coupons, teaspoons, and daily vitamins inside the sack—your table will always be set for a comforting cup of tea. It's easy to make, just sew a basic bag from fabric, shape it with fabric stiffener, then trim with appliqués. For a honey of a gift, fill the sack with special teas and tuck in a teddy bear honey bottle.

YOU WILL NEED

- 14" × 18½" (35.5 × 47cm) piece of sunflower print fabric
- Liquid fabric stiffener
- Self-sealing plastic bag
- 9" × 13" (23 × 33cm) piece of paper-backed fusible web
- 5" × 10" (13 × 25.5cm) piece of gold print fabric, for honey jar appliqué
- 7" × 10" (18 × 25.5cm) piece of fusible fleece
- 4" × 8" (10 × 20.5cm) piece of yellow print fabric, for jar top appliqué
- 2" × 3" (5 × 7.5cm) piece of cream print fabric
- 4" × 5" (10 × 13cm) piece of black print fabric, for bees
- ⅜ yd (34.5cm) of ribbon, ⅛" (3mm) wide
- 4" × 4½" (10 × 11.5cm) piece of yellow print fabric
- 1" × 4" (2.5 × 10cm) block of floral foam
- Assorted dried flowers
- 5" (12.5cm) square wicker basket
- ¾ yd (68.5m) of green floral wire

MAKE THE SACK

① Cut an 11¼" × 18½" (28.5 × 47cm) piece of sunflower print fabric. Set aside the remaining sunflower fabric to use for the sunflower appliqué.

② Fold the fabric in half crosswise with right sides together. Sew each side in a ¼" (6mm) seam.

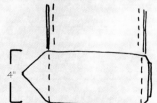

③ Fold the sack to sew a 4" (10cm) long seam across each bottom corner. Trim the seam allowances to ¼" (6mm).

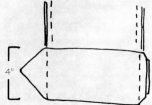

4"

4 Turn the sack right side out. Fold under a 1¾" (4.5cm) hem around the top of the sack.

5 Pour liquid fabric stiffener into a self-sealing plastic bag. Place the sack in the bag and seal. Knead the sack until the fabric is saturated.

6 Open the bag, and pull out the sack with one hand while squeezing excess stiffener into the bag with the other hand.

7 Blot the sack lightly with paper towels to remove excess stiffener. Stand the sack on waxed paper. Stuff the sack with several crumpled pieces of waxed paper to support the sides.

8 Let the sack dry for several hours, or until barely damp. Remove the waxed paper. Crease the side edges of the sack between your fingers. Smooth any wrinkles out of the sack, then stuff the sack with fresh waxed paper. Let the sack dry completely.

MAKE APPLIQUÉS

⑨ Trace one honey jar, one honey label, and one jar top pattern onto the paper side of paper-backed fusible web.

⑩ Cut out each tracing roughly, leaving a small margin of web around the outline. Cut the gold print, yellow print, and sunflower print appliqué fabrics in half. Position each tracing, web side down, on the wrong side of one piece of appliqué fabric. Follow the web manufacturer's instructions to apply the web. Cut out each pattern shape on the traced outline. Cut 2 printed sunflower motifs from the fused fabric.

⑪ Do not remove the paper backings.

⑫ Cut a piece of fusible fleece the same size as each remaining piece of matching appliqué fabric. Follow manufacturer's instructions to fuse the fleece to the wrong side of the fabric, keeping the edges even.

⑬ Remove the paper backing from the appliqués. Fuse each appliqué to the fleece side of the fabrics. Cut around each appliqué outline through all layers.

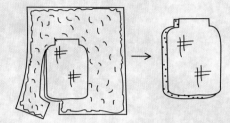

⑭ Prepare the following plain appliqués in same manner as padded appliqués, but omit the fleece. Remove the paper backing from the appliqué, and fuse it to the wrong side of the remaining appliqué fabric. Make 3 bee heads from gold print and 3 bee bodies from black print. Make 3 bee wings and 2 reversed bee wings from yellow print.

⑮ Use a black marker to draw tiny dashes or Xs along the edges of each appliqué to create the look of stitches.

⑯ Use the pattern paint lines and photograph as a guide to draw the remaining details on each appliqué. Draw a nose and an eye on each bee head. Write "HONEY" on the label. Outline with Xs.

ASSEMBLE BASKET

⑰ Peel the paper backing off the label to fuse it to the center of the jar. Fold the jar top, and glue it over the jar.

⑱ Wrap the ribbon around the jar top and tie into a bow. Trim the ribbon ends diagonally. Glue the appliqué sunflowers over the bow.

⑲ Use old scissors to cut the basket in half. Glue floral foam inside one half and glue it to the front of the sack. Glue the jar to the front of the sack, just above the basket. Glue a bee head and 1 or 2 wings onto each bee body.

⑳ Cut 4", 8", and 15" (10, 20, and 38cm) pieces of floral wire. Wrap the longest piece around the black marker to form a coil. Slip coil off the marker. Glue one end of each remaining wire to the back of a bee. Glue the other end of each wire onto the floral foam. Glue the dried flowers into the floral foam.

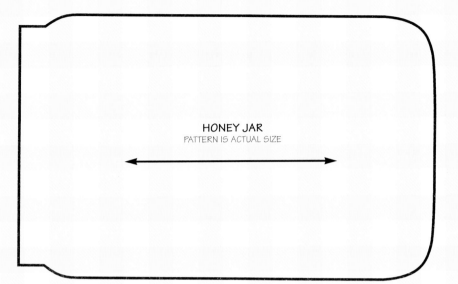

HONEY JAR
PATTERN IS ACTUAL SIZE

HONEY JAR LABEL
PATTERN IS ACTUAL SIZE

HoNEY

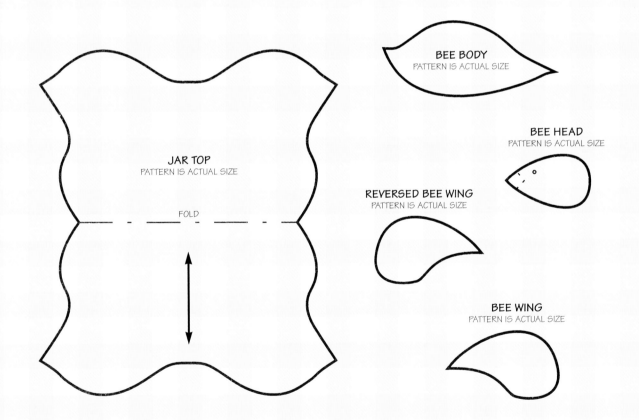

JAR TOP
PATTERN IS ACTUAL SIZE

FOLD

BEE BODY
PATTERN IS ACTUAL SIZE

BEE HEAD
PATTERN IS ACTUAL SIZE

REVERSED BEE WING
PATTERN IS ACTUAL SIZE

BEE WING
PATTERN IS ACTUAL SIZE

Fabric Foldie Covered Tin

This fabric-covered container is as handy for keeping home-baked goodies fresh as it is for keeping sewing tools together. Although it looks as if it's made with an old pieced quilting technique, it's actually made with an easy cut, fold, and glue project called "foldies." The designs are formed by arranging folded fabric circles in a circle around the top of a round metal storage tin. Add a felt lining to make a padded hideaway for jewelry and other keepsakes.

Layered Blues

YOU WILL NEED

- ¾ yd (68.5cm) of light blue printed fabric
- 4" × 7½" (10 × 19cm) tin with lid
- ¼ yd (23cm) of light blue fabric
- ¼ yd (23cm) of medium blue fabric
- 1½ yds (1.4m) of white loop edging, ½" (1.5cm) wide
- 2¾ yds (2.5m) of light blue single fold bias tape, ½" (1.5cm) wide
- 3 sheets of self-stick felt (optional)

TRY THIS!

To line the tin with felt, you may need to use more than one sheet of self-stick felt to cut each section. Line up the edges and treat the pieces as one.

COVER THE TIN

① Use light blue print fabric to cover the tin. Measure around the outside of the tin, then add ½" (1.5cm). Measure the depth of the tin up to the lip where the lid rests, then add ½" (1.5cm). Cut a fabric strip to these measurements.

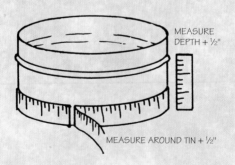

MEASURE DEPTH + ½"

MEASURE AROUND TIN + ½"

② Turn under both long fabric edges ¼" (6mm) and glue. Glue the fabric around the tin, turning the raw end under ½" (1.5cm).

③ Measure the lid up one side, across the top, and down the other side, then add 1" (2.5cm). Cut a fabric square to this measurement.

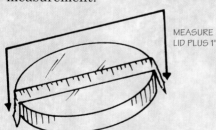

MEASURE LID PLUS 1"

4 Fold the fabric square into quarters. Draw a curved cutting line from one corner diagonally across to another corner. Cut on this line. Unfold the fabric.

5 Center the fabric on the lid. Glue it to the top of the lid. Clip the fabric at the sides up to the top of the lid. Overlap clipped fabric and glue.

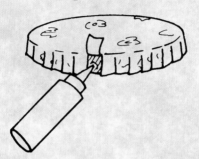

6 Let glue dry. Use a craft knife to trim the fabric even with the bottom edge of the lid.

MAKE FOLDIES

7 Cut circle pattern from these fabrics: 12 from blue print, 8 from light blue, and 8 from medium blue.

⑧ With wrong sides together, fold fabric circles in half. Glue the raw edges together.

⑨ For layered foldies, stack 3 half-circles in 3 colors. Fold the edges to the center. Glue the raw edges together. Make 4 layered foldies.

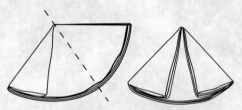

⑩ For basic foldies, fold each of the remaining half-circles in half to make quarter-circles. Glue folds in place.

⑪ Arrange the layered foldies on the lid so that their points meet at the center. Glue the edges to the lid. Let glue dry.

⑫ To make a star, glue 4 light blue basic foldies face up on the lid.

⑬ Arrange 4 medium blue foldies face down on the lid. Stagger the points between points on the first layer. Glue the raw edges to the lid.

⑭ Glue 4 more blue print foldies face down on the lid in the same way. Glue the remaining layers of foldies in the same way.

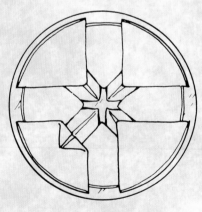

TRIM THE TIN

⑮ Glue loop edging around the top of the lid about ½" (1.5cm) in from the edge and covering the raw edges of the foldies. Butt the ends of the edging, and glue.

⑯ Glue bias tape around the top of the lid, lapping it over the loop edging. Butt the ends of the tape and glue.

⑰ Glue bias tape around the sides of the lid. Butt the ends of the tape and glue.

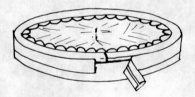

⑱ Measure around the outside of the tin. Cut 1 piece of bias tape and 1 piece of loop edging to this measurement. Glue the loop edging about ¼" (6mm) from the bottom of the tin. Butt the ends and glue.

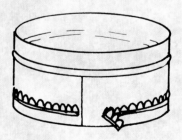

⑲ Glue the bias tape around the bottom edge of the tin, lapping it over the loop edging. Butt the ends of the tape and glue.

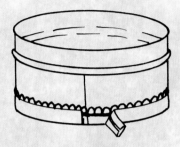

MAKE A LINING

⑳ Take the lid off the tin. Sit the tin on the paper-backed self-stick felt. Trace around the bottom of the tin. Cut out the felt on the traced line.

㉑ Peel the backing off the felt. Press the sticky side of the felt onto the bottom of the tin, smoothing the felt from the center out to eliminate air bubbles. Measure inside height of the tin, and subtract ⅛" (3mm). Measure around the outside circumference of the tin. Cut a strip of felt to each of these measurements.

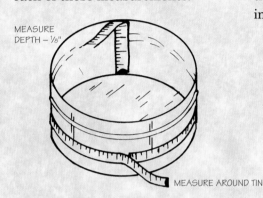

MEASURE DEPTH – ⅛"

MEASURE AROUND TIN

㉒ Peel the backing off one short end of the strip. Stick the felt to the inside of the tin. Peel the backing off as you continue to stick the felt inside the tin. Place the lid on the paper backing of the felt. Trace around the edge of the lid. Cut out the felt just inside the pencil line. Peel off the backing to stick the felt to the inside of the lid.

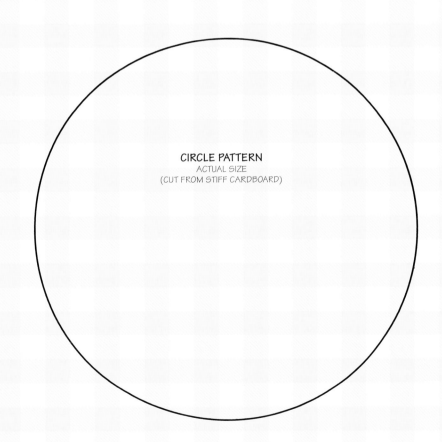

CIRCLE PATTERN
ACTUAL SIZE
(CUT FROM STIFF CARDBOARD)

Twice Remembered

Remember someone special with a photograph "picture frame" that celebrates them twice—once in a small photo, then again with three-dimensional miniatures of their favorite things. Gather dollhouse miniatures, fabrics, and dried flowers. Add other small things that come to mind when you think about the person. It's a wonderful way to recognize a hobby, remember a special occasion, or mark family milestones with a unique, handcrafted gift.

Gardener Glorious

YOU WILL NEED

- 8" × 10" (20.5 × 25.5cm) picture frame
- 2" × 3" (5 × 7.5cm) picture frame
- Paintbrush
- Green acrylic paint
- 8" × 10" (20.5 × 25.5cm) piece of paper-backed fusible web
- Pieces of green mini check fabric: 8" × 10" (20.5 × 25.5cm) and 6" (15cm) square
- Assorted small dried flowers
- 1 yd (91.5cm) of yellow satin ribbon, ⅛" (3mm) wide
- Clear glue for wood, metal, glass, and plastic
- About 5 sprigs of dried baby's breath
- 2" × 3" (5 × 7.5cm) photograph
- 3" (7.5cm) straw basket with handle
- 1½" (4cm) straw hat
- Miniatures such as a watering can, a pitchfork, a hoe, a shovel, 12 vegetables, and a seed bin

PAINT THE FRAMES

① Remove glass and cardboard backing from both frames. Paint both frames. Let paint dry.

MAKE THE SCENE

② Following manufacturer's directions, fuse paper-backed web to the wrong side of the 8" × 10" (20.5 × 25.5cm) fabric. Peel off the paper backing to fuse the fabric to the larger frame's cardboard back.

ABOUT FRAMES

- You will need a large and small picture frame for each project. Select frames that have removable glass and a cardboard backing. Before reassembling each frame to complete the project, clean the glass to remove any fingerprints.

- The smaller frame holds the picture of the subject. For best results, use a photograph that can be trimmed to 2" × 3" (5 × 7.5cm).

CRAFTER'S TIP

Miniature items scaled for dollhouses (one inch equals one foot) work well in these frames.

③ Reserve small sprig of dried flowers to trim the hat. Arrange remaining flowers into 2 bouquets. Trim the stems if necessary so that bouquets are about 3" (7.5cm) long. Cut two 9" (23cm) pieces of yellow ribbon. Tie a ribbon in a bow around each bouquet. Glue bows to bouquets to secure. Arrange dried baby's breath and remaining small flowers in a loose spray on the right-hand side of the fabric-covered cardboard. Trim the sprigs and

flower stems to size if necessary. Glue arrangement in place.

④ Fold the fabric square to line the basket, and glue to the inside of the basket. Glue vegetables inside the basket. Tie remaining yellow ribbon in a bow around crown of straw hat. Glue a small sprig of dried flowers to the hat behind the bow.

FRAME THE SCENE

⑤ Reassemble the large frame by replacing the glass and cardboard. Reassemble the small

frame by replacing the glass, inserting the photograph, and replacing the cardboard. Glue the small frame to the glass of the large frame. Glue the bouquets and miniatures to the large frame.

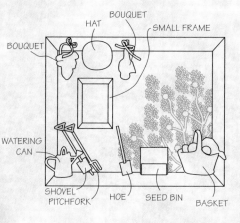

What's Cooking?

YOU WILL NEED

- 8" × 10" (20.5 × 25.5cm) picture frame
- 2" × 3" (5 × 7.5cm) picture frame
- 2" × 3" (5 × 7.5cm) photograph
- Blue/white linen dish towel
- Paintbrush
- Acrylic paint in blue and terra-cotta
- 8" × 10" (20.5 × 25.5cm) piece of paper-backed fusible web
- Clear glue for wood, metal, glass, and plastic
- Miniatures of fruits, a round table, a wooden bucket, 2 blue speckle pots, and a 5" (13cm) broom
- Half of a walnut shell
- 2" × 4½" (5 × 11.5cm) piece of cloud-print wrapping paper
- 2" × 4½" (5 × 11.5cm) dollhouse window
- 7" (18cm) of red yarn

MAKE THE SCENE

1 See Gardener Glorious to paint the frames and make the scene. Paint the large frame blue and the small frame terra-cotta.

2 Cut an 8" × 10" (20.5 × 25.5cm) piece of dish towel to fuse to the large frame's cardboard backing. Glue miniature fruit into walnut shell, reserving 1 pear. Glue the walnut shell to the round table. Slide blue paper behind clear acetate of dollhouse window. Glue the reserved miniature pear to the right-hand corner of the windowsill. Tie yarn in a bow around broom handle.

FRAME THE SCENE

3 See Gardener Glorious to frame the scene. Glue the small frame, the window, the bucket, and a pot to the glass of the large frame. Glue the remaining miniatures to the frame.

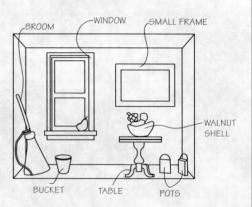

Potpourri Sachet

In days gone by, a lady would tuck a sweet-scented hankie into her bodice or a child might tie up her few pennies of spending money in the corner of a hankie. When we see handkerchiefs today, so many associations come with them that the little scrap of fabric is almost poetry. A fragrant potpourri-filled handkerchief, stitched with the message of a special flower, will bring a touch of old-fashioned romance to your dresser top or pillow.

YOU WILL NEED

- White tulle
- Handkerchief
- Embroidery hoop
- Embroidery ribbon and floss (see Flower Embroider Design for colors)
- Embroidery needle: chenille, crewel, or tapestry
- Terrycloth towel
- Spray starch
- Handful of polyester fiberfill
- Handful of potpourri
- 18" (45.5cm) of ribbon or cord, ⅛" (3mm) wide

TRANSFER DESIGN AND MAKE A SACHET

① Place tulle over the desired flower embroidery pattern. Trace black dots from pattern onto netting with disappearing marker. Place tulle on right side of hankerchief. Trace over dots with disappearing ink marker. Remove tulle before stitching.

② To embroider flowers on one hankie corner, place fabric in an embroidery hoop with transferred design face up. Thread 10" (25.5cm) to 16" (40.5cm) of ribbon into an embroidery needle, needle must be large enough for the ribbon to lay flat when threaded.

③ Embroider the design, using the stitch symbols on each pattern to find corresponding stitches in the Stitch Guide. Use your thumb or a blunt needle to adjust the ribbon as you stitch. For most stitches, the ribbon must be kept flat and smooth. If desired, untwist the ribbon during each stitch and

CRAFTER'S TIP

To keep ribbon from slipping out of needle, begin with a needle lock stitch. Thread ribbon through needle eye. Pierce short end of ribbon about ¼" (6mm) from end. Pull long end until ribbon is firmly locked on needle.

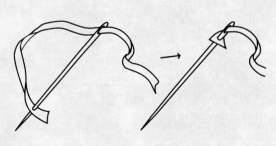

To center the embroidery design on the hankie corner, fold hankie in half diagonally. Fold again into quarters. Finger press fold and open hankie. Line up centering line on embroidery design with the fold at one corner.

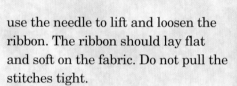

use the needle to lift and loosen the ribbon. The ribbon should lay flat and soft on the fabric. Do not pull the stitches tight.

④ When you finish each flower or small area, knot the ribbon on the wrong side of your needlework to keep the stitch in place. Trim off extra ribbon. Do not leave fabric in hoop if you put your work aside for a few hours.

⑤ When you've finished your ribbon embroidery, remove it from hoop. Press face down on a terrycloth towel to avoid flattening the stitches. If desired, mist embroidered area with water on the right side to fluff the stitches.

⑥ Use spray starch to press embroidered hankie face down on a terrycloth towel. Then, put hankie right side down on your work surface. Make a ball of fiberfill about the size of a golf ball. If your hankie is extra big, make a bigger ball. Center fiberfill ball on hankie. Use your finger to make a hole in the fiberfill center. Fill the hole with potpourri.

⑦ Fold up corners. Fold embroidered corner last so that it will be on top. Tie ribbon or cord to gather hankie over the fiberfill ball.

FLOWERS AND THEIR MEANINGS

Make gifts your family or friends will treasure. Stitch a flower to symbolize a special month, message, or personality.

MONTH	FLOWER	TRADITIONAL MEANING
January	Carnation	Deep Emotion
February	Violet	Faithfulness
March	Hyacinth	Playfulness
April	Sweet Pea	Delicate Pleasures
May	Lily of the Valley	Return of Happiness
June	Rose	Love
July	Larkspur	Light-heartedness
August	Gladiolus	Strength of Character
September	Aster	Variety
October	Marigold	Hope
November	Chrysanthemum	Truth
December	Narcissus	Self-love

Embroidery Stitch Guide

FRENCH KNOT

Bring the needle and ribbon up through the fabric and wrap the ribbon around needle 3 times. Insert the needle close to starting point, then pull down. Knot the ribbon under the fabric to finish.

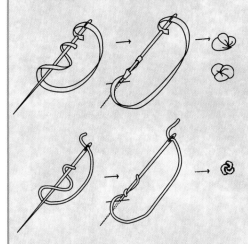

LOOP STITCH

Bring the needle and ribbon up through fabric. Push the needle down about 1/8" (3mm) from the entry point. Use your thumb to hold the ribbon tight as you pull it through and form a loop. Hold loop in place with your thumb or a blunt needle and bring the needle back up through ribbon at the base of the loop.

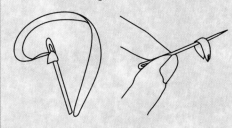

STEM STITCH

Bring the needle and the ribbon up through the fabric. Make one slightly slanted stitch. For the next stitch, bring the needle up at the center and just to the side of the previous stitch.

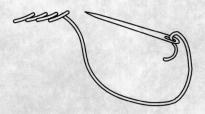

PISTIL STITCH

Bring the needle and the ribbon up through fabric. Make a stitch of the desired length, insert needle and pull floss down. Make one French knot (left) at outer end of straight stitch.

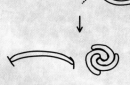

RIBBON STITCH

Bring the needle and the ribbon up through fabric. Lay the ribbon flat on the fabric. At the end of the stitch, pierce the ribbon with the needle. Gently pull ribbon through, allowing the ribbon to curl at the tip. Pull the ribbon through slowly to avoid making stitch too tight.

STRAIGHT STITCH

Bring the needle and the ribbon up through fabric. Make a stitch of the desired length, insert the needle and pull the ribbon down.

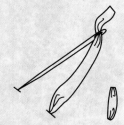

FEATHER STITCH

Bring the needle and the ribbon up through fabric. Make a straight stitch (above) angled to one side, leaving the floss loose. Bring the needle up through the fabric below center of stitch. Pull ribbon down to form a round V and insert the needle to hold in place. Make a second straight stitch toward the other side. Continue, alternating straight stitches to the left and right.

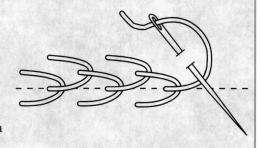

SPIDER WEB ROSE

Bring the needle and the ribbon up through fabric and make a straight stitch (page 121), leaving ribbon loose enough to make a loop.

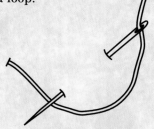

Push the needle down through fabric and back up so that it passes through the loop and over ribbon or floss. Insert needle down through the fabric to form a Y. Continue making stitches to form 5 spokes.

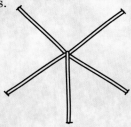

Thread the needle with the darkest shade of ribbon for the center. Bring needle and the ribbon up through the fabric at the center of the spokes and turn the needle a few times to twist ribbon. Weave ribbon loosely, over and under spokes, pushing rows together as you weave. Use the medium shade for the middle third and the lightest shade for the outer third of the rose.

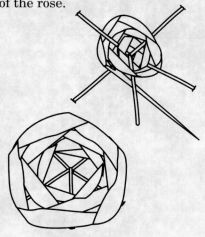

EMBROIDERY FLOSS COLOR KEY

See each flower embroidery design for colors needed. Use 2 strands of floss.

COLOR	DMC	COATS	ANCHOR
Lime green	471	6010	265
Pale green	563	6210	208
Bright green	988	6258	243
Kelly green	704	6238	238
Forest green	937	6268	268
Yellow green	472	6253	264
Yellow	725	2298	305
Lemon yellow	727	2289	293
Orange	721	2324	324
Pink	605	3001	50

EMBROIDERY RIBBON COLOR KEY

See each flower embroidery design for colors needed.
All ribbons are 4mm except where noted.

COLOR	SILK		SYNTHETIC
	YLI	BUCILLA	MOKUBA
Pale green	31	618	356
Bright green	19	638	340
Dark green 4mm & 7mm	20	628	366
Kelly green	60	642	357
Light purple	83	024	182
Lemon yellow	119	655	429
Yellow	120	656	409
Yellow gold	121	666	424
Pink	122	544	004
Coral	123	541	044
Light blue	124	459	293
Dark blue	126	252	252
Rose	128	553	013
Light brown	139	668	136
Gold	147	668	431
Bronze	148	524	136
Spice	149	511	118
Bight pink	152	552	052
Light green	154	509	367
Ivory 4mm & 7mm	156	501	470
Mauve	157	531	074
Lime green	170	648	364
Forest green	171	643	379
Orange	174	512	124
Purple	177	113	160
Lavender	178	198	161

Flower Embroidery Designs

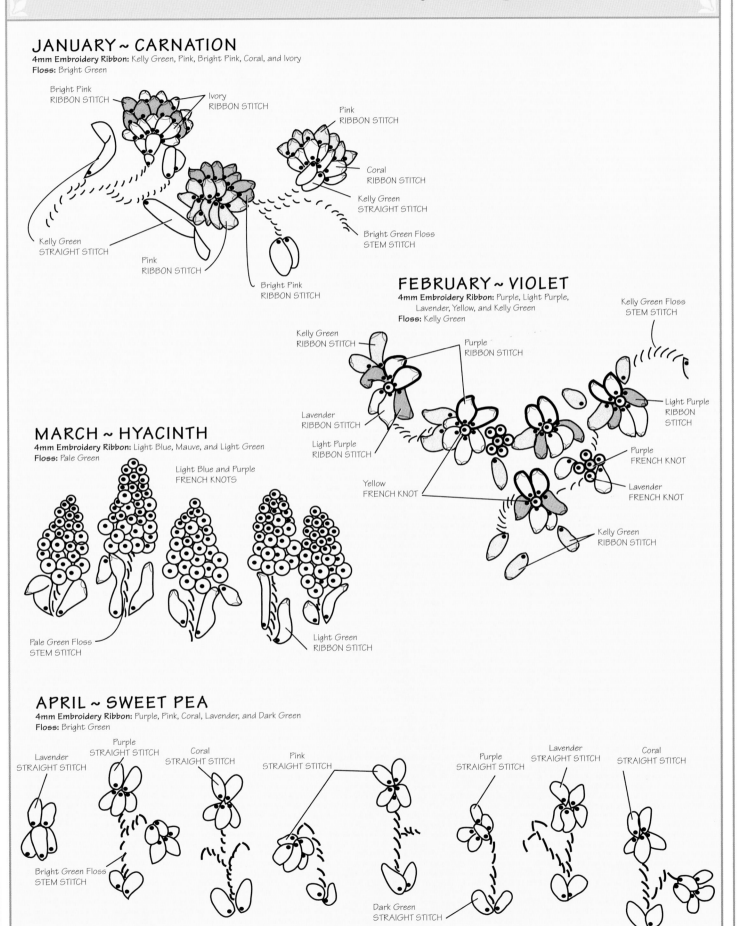

JANUARY ~ CARNATION
4mm Embroidery Ribbon: Kelly Green, Pink, Bright Pink, Coral, and Ivory
Floss: Bright Green

Bright Pink
RIBBON STITCH

Ivory
RIBBON STITCH

Pink
RIBBON STITCH

Coral
RIBBON STITCH

Kelly Green
STRAIGHT STITCH

Bright Green Floss
STEM STITCH

Kelly Green
STRAIGHT STITCH

Pink
RIBBON STITCH

Bright Pink
RIBBON STITCH

FEBRUARY ~ VIOLET
4mm Embroidery Ribbon: Purple, Light Purple, Lavender, Yellow, and Kelly Green
Floss: Kelly Green

Kelly Green
RIBBON STITCH

Purple
RIBBON STITCH

Kelly Green Floss
STEM STITCH

Lavender
RIBBON STITCH

Light Purple
RIBBON STITCH

Light Purple
RIBBON STITCH

Yellow
FRENCH KNOT

Purple
FRENCH KNOT

Lavender
FRENCH KNOT

Kelly Green
RIBBON STITCH

MARCH ~ HYACINTH
4mm Embroidery Ribbon: Light Blue, Mauve, and Light Green
Floss: Pale Green

Light Blue and Purple
FRENCH KNOTS

Pale Green Floss
STEM STITCH

Light Green
RIBBON STITCH

APRIL ~ SWEET PEA
4mm Embroidery Ribbon: Purple, Pink, Coral, Lavender, and Dark Green
Floss: Bright Green

Lavender
STRAIGHT STITCH

Purple
STRAIGHT STITCH

Coral
STRAIGHT STITCH

Pink
STRAIGHT STITCH

Purple
STRAIGHT STITCH

Lavender
STRAIGHT STITCH

Coral
STRAIGHT STITCH

Bright Green Floss
STEM STITCH

Dark Green
STRAIGHT STITCH

MAY ~ LILY OF THE VALLEY
7mm Embroidery Ribbon: Ivory and Dark Green
Floss: Bright Green

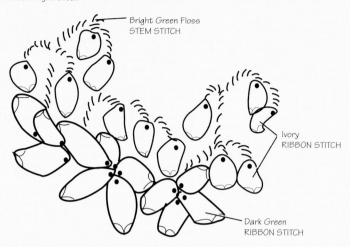

Bright Green Floss
STEM STITCH

Ivory
RIBBON STITCH

Dark Green
RIBBON STITCH

JUNE ~ ROSE
4mm Embroidery Ribbon: Yellow, Bright Green, Pale Green, Lavender, Purple, Bright Pink, Pink, and Rose

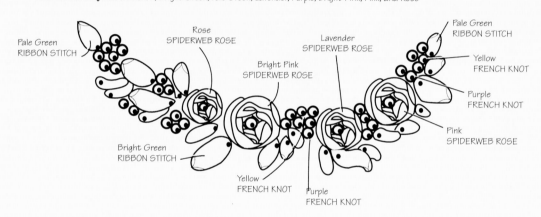

Pale Green
RIBBON STITCH

Rose
SPIDERWEB ROSE

Lavender
SPIDERWEB ROSE

Pale Green
RIBBON STITCH

Bright Pink
SPIDERWEB ROSE

Yellow
FRENCH KNOT

Purple
FRENCH KNOT

Bright Green
RIBBON STITCH

Pink
SPIDERWEB ROSE

Yellow
FRENCH KNOT

Purple
FRENCH KNOT

JULY ~ LARKSPUR
4mm Embroidery Ribbon: Pink, Coral, Purple, and Forest Green
Floss: Lime Green and Lemon Yellow

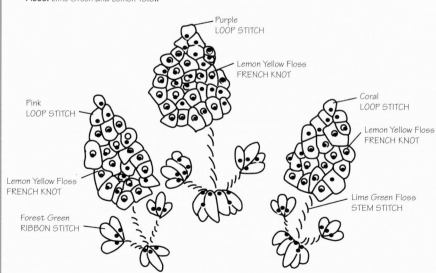

Purple
LOOP STITCH

Lemon Yellow Floss
FRENCH KNOT

Pink
LOOP STITCH

Coral
LOOP STITCH

Lemon Yellow Floss
FRENCH KNOT

Lemon Yellow Floss
FRENCH KNOT

Forest Green
RIBBON STITCH

Lime Green Floss
STEM STITCH

AUGUST ~ GLADIOLUS
4mm Embroidery Ribbon: Lime Green and Yellow Gold
Floss: Yellow Green and Orange

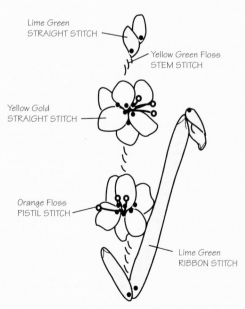

Lime Green
STRAIGHT STITCH

Yellow Green Floss
STEM STITCH

Yellow Gold
STRAIGHT STITCH

Orange Floss
PISTIL STITCH

Lime Green
RIBBON STITCH

SEPTEMBER ~ ASTER
4mm Embroidery Ribbon: Light Blue, Light Purple, Mauve, and Dark Blue
Floss: Pale Green and Lemon Yellow

Pale Green Floss
FEATHER STITCH

Lemon
Yellow Floss
FRENCH KNOTS
(2 wraps of
2 strands)

Lemon
Yellow Floss
FRENCH KNOTS
(2 wraps of
2 strands)

Mauve
RIBBON
STITCH

Light Purple
RIBBON
STITCH

Dark Blue
RIBBON
STITCH

Light Blue
RIBBON
STITCH

Mauve
RIBBON
STITCH

Pale Green
Floss
FEATHER
STITCH

OCTOBER ~ MARIGOLD
4mm Embroidery Ribbon: Forest Green, Yellow Gold, and Spice
Floss: Forest Green and Yellow Gold

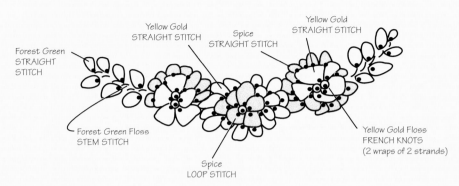

Yellow Gold
STRAIGHT STITCH

Spice
STRAIGHT STITCH

Yellow Gold
STRAIGHT STITCH

Forest Green
STRAIGHT
STITCH

Forest Green Floss
STEM STITCH

Spice
LOOP STITCH

Yellow Gold Floss
FRENCH KNOTS
(2 wraps of 2 strands)

NOVEMBER ~ CHRYSANTHEMUM
4mm Embroidery Ribbon: Forest Green, Bronze, Gold, Light Brown, and Ivory
Floss: Lime Green

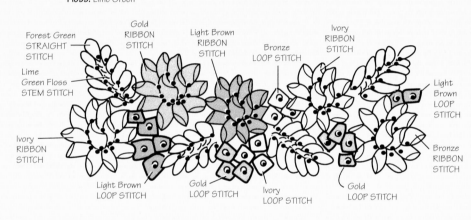

Forest Green
STRAIGHT
STITCH

Gold
RIBBON
STITCH

Light Brown
RIBBON
STITCH

Bronze
LOOP STITCH

Ivory
RIBBON
STITCH

Lime
Green Floss
STEM STITCH

Light
Brown
LOOP
STITCH

Ivory
RIBBON
STITCH

Bronze
RIBBON
STITCH

Light Brown
LOOP STITCH

Gold
LOOP STITCH

Ivory
LOOP STITCH

Gold
LOOP STITCH

DECEMBER ~ NARCISSUS
4mm Embroidery Ribbon: Ivory, Dark Green, Orange, Spice, and Yellow Gold
7mm Embroidery Ribbon: Ivory and Dark Green

4mm Dark Green
STRAIGHT
STITCH

4mm Ivory
STRAIGHT STITCH

4mm Dark Green
TWISTED
STRAIGHT STITCH

4mm Dark
Green
STRAIGHT
STITCH

Spice
FRENCH
KNOT

Yellow Gold
LOOP STITCH

7mm Ivory
LOOP STITCH

4mm Ivory
STRAIGHT
STITCH

7mm Dark
Green
RIBBON STITCH

Spice
FRENCH KNOT

4mm Ivory
FRENCH KNOT

4mm Ivory
FRENCH KNOT

Orange
LOOP STITCH

7mm Dark Green
RIBBON STITCH

Yellow Gold
LOOP STITCH

7mm Dark Green
STRAIGHT STITCH

Sources

A wonderful selection of materials and supplies can be found at your favorite fabric or craft store, such as ABC Fabrics, Cloth World, Crafts 'n More, Hancock Fabrics, House of Fabrics, JoAnn Fabrics & Crafts, Michael's, A.C. Moore, and Rag Shops.

You may also order craft supplies by mail from the following:

Craft Catalog
P.O. Box 1069
Reynoldsburg, OH 43068
800-777-1442
800-955-5915 Fax
Free catalog

Craft King Discount
   Craft Supply
P.O. Box 90637
Lakeland, FL 33804
800-769-9494
Free catalog

Creative Wholesale
P.O. 2070
Stockbridge, GA 30281
800-347-0930
Free catalog

CR's Crafts
Box 8
Leland, IA 50453
(515) 567-3652

Factory Direct Craft Supply
P.O. Box 16
Franklin, OH 45005
800-252-LACE
Free catalog

Home-Sew
P.O. Box 4099
Bethlehem, PA 18018-0099
(610) 867-3833

Nancy's Notions
P.O. Box 683
Beaver Dam, WI 53916-0683
800-833-0690
Free catalog

Suncoast Discount
   Arts & Crafts
9015 US19 North
Pinellas Park, FL 34666
(813) 572-1600
Catalog $2

Index